# Renewed Survival

# Renewed Survival

## Jewish Community Life in Croatia

Nila Ginger Hofman

LEXINGTON BOOKS

A division of
ROWMAN & LITTLEFIELD PUBLISHERS, INC.
*Lanham • Boulder • New York • Toronto • Oxford*

LEXINGTON BOOKS

A division of Rowman & Littlefield Publishers, Inc.
A wholly owned subsidiary of The Rowman & Littlefield Publishing Group, Inc.
4501 Forbes Boulevard, Suite 200
Lanham, MD 20706

PO Box 317
Oxford
OX2 9RU, UK

British Library Cataloguing in Publication Information Available

**Library of Congress Cataloging-in-Publication Data**

Hofman, Nila Ginger, 1962–
    Renewed survival : Jewish community life in Croatia / Nila Ginger Hofman.
        p.   cm.
    Includes bibliographical references and index.
    ISBN 0–7391–1329–1 (cloth : alk. paper)—ISBN 0–7391–1330–5 (pbk. : alk. paper)
    1. Jews—Croatia—History.  2. Jews—Croatia—Identity.  3. Jews—Croatia—
Zagreb—History.  4. Yugoslavia—Ethnic relations.  5. Croatia—Ethnic relations.
I. Title.
DS135.C75H64   2006
949.72′004924—dc22                                                     2005023622

Printed in the United States of America

♾ ™ The paper used in this publication meets the minimum requirements of American
National Standard for Information Sciences—Permanence of Paper for Printed Library
Materials, ANSI/NISO Z39.48–1992.

*In Memory of Velimir Hofman*
(1930–1995)

# Contents

# Acknowledgments

Neither gratitude nor words comes close to expressing what the people from the ŽOZ have given me. I owe many of my personal insights in exploring my Jewish background to them. I thank them for their thoughtful suggestions, encouragement, and hospitality. I thank them also for sharing their lives with me and for their friendship. I remain indebted to them for supplying me with part of my heritage. I am particularly grateful to Ruth Betelheim, Dona Danon, Dunja Šprajc, Leila and Marina Šprajc, Dean Friedrich, Zoran Mirković, Mira Wolf, Zoran Babić, Lea Kriesbacher, Vukan Marinković-Šiljo, Sanja Zoričić-Tabaković, Neven Tabaković, Maja Binenfeld, Sonja Makek Bar-Sela, Saša Cvetkovic, Lea Lustig, Hana Vojnic, Ada Lučić, Ana Domaš, Ilan Hadji-Ristić, Neda Wiesler, Vlasta Kovač, Nicola Jovanović, Silvia Heim, Alfred Pal, Julia Koš, Mira Altarac Hadji-Ristić, Luciano Prelević, Jasenka Furst, Ivo Goldstein, and many others to whom I apologize for not mentioning here. Without them, this study would not have been as rich of an experience as it has been.

Taking a couple of steps back, I thank my mother, Odile Hofman Pimpach, for introducing me to the ŽOZ in 1995, after the commemorative funeral held for my father, who had passed away earlier that year. The idea of conducting ethnographic research with Croatian Jews emerged during my initial introduction to the ŽOZ. Andrew Buckser, my dissertation advisor at Purdue University in West Lafayette, Indiana, was the first person who encouraged me to commence the study of Jews in Croatia. I thank him for his guidance and support.

Funding for this study was provided by a number of different sources, including the Memorial Foundation for Jewish Culture and the Purdue Research Foundation, both of which supported my field research in Croatia and the bulk of my dissertation writing in West Lafayette, Indiana. I received additional support for the study during my initial prefieldwork phase from the Purdue Research Foundation. Later, in the postdoctoral phase, I received generous support from three programs at DePaul University in Chicago, Illinois: the Faculty Research Development Program, the University Research Council, and the Liberal Arts & Sciences Research Assistant Program. Many thanks go to my research assistants at DePaul, Maja Ljubanić and Larisa Kurtović, and in Zagreb to Lea Šiljak, who worked diligently on translations and transcriptions and who helped put the "đ," and "č" in all the appropriate places. I especially thank Maja and Larisa for their humor and kindness and Michelle Romanoff for the Hebrew translations.

I am grateful to the staff at the Institute of Folklore in Zagreb and the anthropology department at Zagreb University for allowing me to use their facilities. I thank Tomo Vinšćak, the first anthropologist I met in Zagreb, for his help and introductions. Many thanks go to my colleagues at Purdue, DePaul, and elsewhere who gave me valuable insights and encouragement for this project. Among them are Evelyn Blackwood, Frida Furman, O. Michael Watson, Rebecca Shapiro, and Robert Melson. A very special thanks goes to my good friend Katie Watson for offering her invaluable editorial suggestions. Thanks also go to Michael Schwartz, who assisted Katie in this task. I thank Brian Romer at Rowman & Littlefield who recognized the merit of this project.

I thank my dogs Ullu Wattu—who accompanied me to the field and helped me make many friends in Zagreb—and Naima, who each at their turn sat faithfully next to me and supported me through all the writing and rewriting phases. Finally, my loving gratitude for making this project become a reality goes to John deMoulpied, whose intelligence, meticulous editing and re-editing, persistent love, and emotional support made bearable the many months of separation we had to endure while I was in the field and the many edits in the postdissertation phase.

# Preface

On the southwest corner of *Palmotićeva Ulica*, a few blocks north of Zagreb's bustling *Ban Jelačić Square*, the four-story, flat gray façade of the *Židovska Općina Zagreb* (ŽOZ), the Jewish Community Center, has marked the physical site of Zagreb's Jewish community since 1898. In 1991, following an attempted bombing, a guardhouse was installed to the north of the entrance along *Palmotićeva*; but, apart from this, the exterior of the *općina* has changed little over the past one hundred years. The term *općina* refers to "community" or "municipality" in standard Croatian. However, local ŽOZ affiliates refer to the ŽOZ community center as the *"općina"* when describing the physical community *center* as well as when referring to the more evasive concept of the "Jewish community."

Visitors to the ŽOZ pass by the twenty-four-hour security guard stationed at the guardhouse and then announce their arrival through an intercom. Upon entering, they must pass through an additional series of security checks, positioned just inside the massive steel doors at the ŽOZ's entrance. As foreboding an image as this may conjure, it stands in stark contrast to the warmth and congeniality with which I was welcomed into the *općina* when I began my fieldwork there in 1997.

My fondest memories of the *općina* include the weekly *kaffeklatsch* I shared with my students following our English language class. Each week following class, we retreated to the plush surrounds of the *klub*, a multipurpose room located on the *općina*'s second floor, where we would discuss recipes, politics, and Jewish identity. I would come to discover that the congeniality and openness of my first experiences at the ŽOZ was due, in large measure, to the unique convergence of Croatian Jews and others interested in the community life of the ŽOZ, for which the physical space of the *općina* continues to serve as a focal point.

In many ways, the community life I discovered at the *općina* ran contrary to my expectations. For years, proponents of what I shall call the "disappearance thesis" have argued that the bonds of Jewish community life require religious observance. Accordingly, the largely social bonds that characterize community members' affiliations with the *općina* and one another, together with relatively high rates of intercultural marriages and a marked absence of religious observance, are precisely the sorts of trends that disappearance thesis proponents regard as signaling the decline of the Jewish community. My experiences at the ŽOZ, however, belied this prognostication.

My initial visit to the ŽOZ was not, in the first instance, for the purpose of this study. In 1962 I was born in Zagreb, which at that time was part of Yugoslavia. My parents and I left for the Netherlands when I was four years old. Like many Yugoslavs, we headed west in search of better economic opportunities. I visited my paternal grandmother in Yugoslavia during the hot summer months of 1971–1976 while my parents labored to make a better life for our family in the Netherlands. There, I swam competitively for the local *Mladost* swimming club. Outside of my feverish pool practice (six hours a day), I spent most of my time with my grandmother Štefica. Together we shopped at the central open-air market in downtown Zagreb, met aging relatives at a *slastičarna* (pastry shop), and saw matinees on Saturday afternoons.

Few memories stand out from those days. I recall the tantalizing smells from my grandmother's kitchen when she cooked lunch, the main meal in Croatia. Thinking of the potato parsley soup she made served with a medallion of sour cream in the middle still makes my mouth water. In the mornings, we would eat her homemade preserves and warm bread. Even more vividly, I recall our weekly visits to the Mirogoj cemetery in Zagreb, where my grandfather was buried in 1971.

During those Sunday visits, I sat on the family grave and watched my grandmother pick the vines that grew from beneath the black marble stone. She used to send me to the nearest water pump with a plastic bucket. We used the water to clean the gravestone and to water the flowerpots placed on each side of the grave. When I asked my grandmother why there were six names listed on the grave divided by a Star of David sign and only three people buried, she explained that the names and dates listed on the left of the star were my grandfather's and his parents. The names and dates listed on the right were prefaced by: *spomen poginulih od fašističke ruke* (in memory of those who fell victim to fascist's hands). My eleven-year-old mind struggled with the "hands" part and the death dates behind all the names with no bodies were "1942."

My swimming career ended in 1976, and I spent the remainder of my adolescent summers in the Netherlands. Between 1976 and the beginning of my fieldwork twenty years later, I visited Zagreb on just a few brief occasions.

The last of these occasions (August 1995) was my father's funeral. He had passed away earlier that year in the Netherlands, and his remains where shipped to Croatia and buried in the Jewish section of the Mirogoj cemetery as was his wish. It was during that visit that I first learned about the ŽOZ that would become the site of my fieldwork. My mother asked if I would like to see the place where my father had gone to school, the *općina* of his belonging, and we visited the ŽOZ the day after his funeral. The *općina* would become an important part of my own personal history when I returned to begin my fieldwork in 1997.

While the cemetery visits and the stories my grandmother told of family members who perished in the Holocaust remain vividly engraved in my childhood memory, I did not have a Jewish consciousness before 1993. To this day, I have very little information about my father's Jewish identity. He simply never spoke about what the war, or the Jewish community, meant to him. Religion was also never spoken of at home. We did not go to synagogue or to church. We did not celebrate Christmas or any other Christian holidays. For most of his life, my father was an atheist and the family followed his lead. Then I spent a year studying abroad in Israel. That year was part of the change in my identity.

Israel was full of promise in 1993. The Israelis and the Palestinians had just signed the peace accords. It was during this time of hope that I discovered my relatives in Haifa. Later, a member of the ŽOZ told me that discovering a relative in Israel had enabled her to reconnect with her Jewish heritage. I heard similar stories of reconnecting from many other intercultural Jews I interviewed. Many of the storytellers (as I affectionately call my consultants) are intercultural Jews—people like me who have a Jewish mother, father, or grandparent, and who have grown up without a Jewish consciousness. Their stories, like mine, are about discovering their Jewish heritage as adults. This raised a number of questions that would occupy me for the duration of my research. Why have intercultural Croatian Jews chosen to self-identify as Jews? What other options are available to them? What makes Jewish identity so appealing? How do the politics of time, place, and personal predilections shape and transform a sense of self?

Although the lived realities of Croatian Jews are different than my own, we have experienced similar identity trajectories. We became aware of the changes in our self-perception sometime in the turbulent 1990s. Notwithstanding global shifts in identity politics, the change in the self-perceptions of Croatian Jews is linked to the profound cultural transformation during Croatia's transition from Yugoslavia.

The ŽOZ instantly felt like home. Ever since I first set foot there I knew that I wanted to tell this story. By reworking the lived experiences of ŽOZ members into a cultural analysis of identity, my aim is to present the stories I have been told as documents of historical memory and cultural politics. Inspired by a critical anthropology that ponders questions of representation, the politics of authorship, and self-refection, I have chosen to confront subjects of an anthropological nature that are far from "neutral." Accordingly, I address the process of identity construction and negotiation not by distancing my own views and experiences (as is often customary in social scientific inquiry) but by using those experiences to guide me toward a more meaningful and deeper understanding of the intercultural Jewish identities that emerged from the aftermath of communism.

I realize that my willingness to take on such a risk does not come without a price. To be a self-reflective observer takes skill and guts—*chutzpah*, if you will. In taking such an approach, observers become exposed to questions they may have been afraid to ask. It is in this spirit that I seek to explore my own story and that of my relatives (Jewish and non-Jewish) in terms of the narratives the ŽOZ members entrusted to me.

Along the way, I have taken methodological cues from critical and feminist anthropology by exploring questions of intersubjectivity, the politics of authorship and representation. These ideas transgress *traditional* social scientific inquiry, which advocates distancing one's personal experiences from the subject of inquiry. Susan Krieger (1991) explains that dismissing the experiences of researchers in the context of social science produces contradictory results. As she puts it, "The self—the unique inner life of the observer—is treated as something to be separated out, neutralized, minimized, standardized, and controlled. At the same time, the observer is expected to use the self to the end of understanding the world."

The tension between observer and subject has long been addressed by feminist scholars critical of the methodological underpinnings of traditional social scientific inquiry (Behar and Gordon, 1995; Moore, 1988; Reinharz, 1992; Stacey, 1991; Stack, 1996; Wolf, 1996). For example, Ruth Behar (1996) extends the personal to the realm of the observer's aspiring vulnerability. For Behar, contemporary scholars are increasingly willing to question social scientific objectivity and thus to treat their autobiographical accounts as research data. Accordingly, rather than distancing my personal experiences from the scope of the inquiry, I draw on my personal experiences to guide me towards a more meaningful and deeper understanding of Jewish community life in Croatia.

By exploring the complexities inherent in the renegotiation of Jewish community life, my study contributes to the anthropological literature on the post-communist experience—one in which political and transnational discourses play significant roles (Berdahl, Bunzl, and Lampand, 2000; Burawoy and

Verdery, 1999; Gruber, 2002; Verdery, 1996). It contributes as well to a small but growing literature of Jewish-themed anthropological studies that address the complex sociocultural forces that shape the lives of European Jewry (Buckser, 2003; Bunzl, 2004; Goluboff, 2003; Gordiejew, 1999; Webber, 1994). My work is further aligned with studies that address the experiences of intercultural Jews elsewhere in the world (Azoulay, 1997; Barack Fishman, 2004; Bershtel and Graubard, 1992; Kessel, 2000; Mayer, 1985; Schmelz and DellaPergola, 1988).

## FIRST IMPRESSIONS IN THE FIELD

I was surprised at how unchanged Zagreb seemed when I began my fieldwork in September 1997. Despite the electronic displays of the postcommunist era, the town felt and smelled the same as it did in the 1970s. The bright lights and electronic billboards that surround *Ban Jelačić Square* (once called the *Trg Republike*) gave Zagreb a modern presence. The lovely old trams and cafés, along with the old shoemaker and dressmaker shops I remember from my childhood, all stood in the shadow of the most banal aspects of consumer culture. Businesses such as McDonalds (six locations in Zagreb alone), Vidal Sassoon, and Benetton served as proud symbols of the "new democracy" for some Croatians. This superficial "Westernization" of Croatia was in fact one of the important by-products of the political reforms that took place in the 1990s. Looking beyond the lively cafés and pastry shops, however, I noticed that the names of streets and monuments erected for World War II victims had been either changed or destroyed. I quickly learned that many commercial establishments and streets displayed the names of medieval Croatian kings or else figures that served to align Croatia closer to the West. Name changes such as these were aimed at symbolically opposing Yugoslavism and thereby reimagining the geopolitical position of Croatia. There are many examples of these changes. For example, social critic Slavenka Drakulić (1997) brings attention to a movie theater once called Kino Balkan that has been converted into Kino Europa, thus creating the impression that Croatia belongs to the West. This negation of Yugoslavism and the idealization of Westernization continue to reflect Croatia's desire to join the European Union and to establish free-market capitalism.

Other, not so benign, cultural symbols signaled calls for social order. Drakulić points out that sometime in the mid-1990s, laws against spitting on the sidewalk and hanging one's laundry from street-side balconies were imposed. In a society undergoing rapid socioeconomic and political change, such displays of orderliness served to restrain national chaos in the face of an increasingly visible socioeconomic crisis. Unemployment rates skyrocketed to nearly 20 percent during this period, and that number did not include the 25 percent of able workers who were forced into retirement well before age sixty-five. One might have wondered who was left to constitute a labor force.

During the aftermath of the war in Yugoslavia (1990–1995), when manufacturing jobs dwindled and the tourist industry went into serious decline, few opportunities remained for either young professionals or working class citizens. As the cost of living in Zagreb rose, salaries and retirement pensions either decreased or were simply not paid for months. Laborers and retirees alike recounted stories about not being paid for many months. Despite the promises of the Croatian Democratic Union (*Hrvatska Demokratska Zajednica*, HDZ), the newly formed Croatian nation-state failed to produce a decrease in employment or a higher standard of living. On the contrary, the introduction of free-market political reforms had the reverse effect. Throughout the HDZ's campaign, "democracy" continued to function as a political buzzword, used to disassociate Croatia from the former regime. But just as the Kino Europa is still the same old Kino under a different name, the political rhetoric of democracy and free-market capitalism failed to deliver the freedom it promised.

Soaring unemployment in the years prior to the disintegration of Yugoslavia instilled many with the desire for change. This was reflected in an increased demand for a higher standard of living and for consumer goods that could be bought cheaper abroad. Consumer culture and shopping sprees in neighboring Italy and Austria began to flourish in the late 1960s. Meanwhile, the Yugoslav economy began a slow, downward spiral. Economic migration, often in the form of guest workers migrating to Western Europe, Canada, and the United States, was another response to the local economic conditions. Many claimed to have left for better employment opportunities in the West and out of disillusionment with Josip Broz Tito's self-managing socialism. These transnational migrants believed that Croatia should separate from Yugoslavia. In the 1980s, with the death of Tito, they began organizing in their respective countries of residence and were eventually successful in sponsoring Franjo Tudman's HDZ party, which swept the first national elections in Croatia in 1991. Tudman's victory would soon lead to the separation of Croatia from Yugoslavia—an event that the Diasporic Croats, including my father, had long hoped to see.

In the meantime, Croatia remained caught betwixt and between a vestigial culture of communism and an inchoate free-market capitalism. The standard of living during the time of my fieldwork was at an all-time low and government corruption was rampant. Responding to this trend, disillusioned Croatians voted in a new reform-minded government in the January 2000 elections. The hope for a better and more secure future was reflected in a record-breaking voter turnout (77 percent of the population) and a decisive rejection of HDZ candidates.

Today, President Stjepan Mesić and Prime Minister Ivo Sanader are continuing what Tudman once described as Croatia's one-thousand-year dream of independence. Croatia applied for membership to the European Union in February 2003 and was told that negotiations will commence sometime in 2005. Sanader described these developments as "a great day for Croatia." Of course, the "great day" and the "one-thousand-year dream" are largely symbolic of the enmity toward the East. (Croatia's independence could hardly have been imagined for a millennium, since present day ethnonationalism gained popularity only after the French Revolution.) Rather, what Tudman's "dream" signified was Croatia's economic and political departure from communist Yugoslavia. The idea that Serbs and Croats are, as Tudman once put it, "natural" enemies, and the disillusionment with communism were further emphasized by Tudman's exhortations that Croatia ought to join the Europe where she belongs. Such sentiments coincided with the *orientalization* of Serbs and Bosnian Muslims in Yugoslavia—cultural groups that, in the imagination of their political antagonists, rightfully belong to the East.

The country's struggle to define itself throughout these political transitions is reflected in the lives of Croatian Jews. Many members of the ŽOZ are from so-called mixed marriages—a fact that contributed significantly to their survival during World War II and to the cultural composition of descending generations. The cultural heterogeneity and integration that mark their lives have long-standing roots. Yet with Tudman's exclusivist ethnonationalism, only a small contingency of intercultural religious Jews have experienced the "dilemma" of being viewed as neither Jews nor Croats. For the remainder of the community, rather than constituting a dilemma, exclusion from an *authentic* Croatian identity has made Jewish cultural identity even more appealing. Even though cultural designations such as "Croat" and "minority" are viewed as mutually exclusive categories, the experience of intercultural Jews does not support this. Indeed, for intercultural Jews, such designations represent options (rather than restrictions) amongst a wide-ranging menu of identities available to them.

Archival materials indicate that Jewish clubs and organizations that existed in Croatia from the mid-nineteenth century until 1941 had Jewish as well as non-Jewish members. In Zagreb, membership in such organizations was an important forum through which Jews and non-Jews interacted both socially and politically. Membership in Jewish voluntary associations during the nineteenth century also served to promote the social and political advancement of

Croatian Jews who were excluded from organizations reserved for gentiles. During the resistance movement in World War II, Jews and non-Jewish Croatians fought side by side against the *Ustašas* and the German occupation.

Those who identified as communists during Yugoslavia, identify as antifascists today. Holocaust Remembrance Day is an occasion for many formerly persecuted minorities to connect with one another through shared political ideology. Other evidence points to longstanding cultural integration between non-Jews and Jews in Croatia—for example, while the standard practice in Eastern Europe in the eighteenth century was to have separate cemeteries for Jews and gentiles, Mirogoj, which was built in the eighteenth century, has a "Jewish section." After World War II, cultural integration became an even more significant reality for Croatian Jews, given the diminished pool of *authentic* Jewish marriageable partners (Croatia lost nearly 80 percent of its original Jewish population during the Holocaust).

The Jewish community was further diminished in the late 1940s and early 1950s as a result of massive emigration to Israel and the United States. Since 1952, the number of Jews living in Croatia has remained fairly stable. This might be taken to imply that the number of community members that have passed away is roughly equal to the number of new members that have arrived. There is, however, a more accurate explanation for this relative stability. While there were approximately 1,300 Jews reported living in Zagreb in 1952, the Jewish community now has approximately 1,500 members. Though these numbers do not coincide exactly with national census data (which fluctuate in ethnic and religious affiliation from 1953–2001), there has been an undeniable increase (about 14 percent) in ŽOZ membership since the mid 1990s. This means that more individuals are beginning to claim their Jewish cultural heritage. It also signifies that Jewish identity and ŽOZ membership criteria have been altered.

About half of the registered ŽOZ members share their membership with other members of their households. The 1986 membership reforms, which allowed non-Jewish family members as well as individuals with at least one Jewish grandparent to be registered in the ŽOZ, help to explain this trend. However, many ŽOZ participants are not registered members and some ŽOZ members do not participate in *općina* functions. These figures suggest that participation in community activities is desirable for a number of non-Jewish Croatians. Other demographic data show that the Jewish community in Zagreb is aging, but not as rapidly as has been supposed by those predicting its disintegration. Only one-third of the community members (roughly five hundred individuals) are in the senior (sixty-one years and older) category, and many intercultural Jews, who had been dormant members, became active in the 1990s. Furthermore, a small but rising number of conversions have been taking place since the arrival of the community rabbi in 1998. The newly established school (2003) for first through twelfth grades will further mark these changes.

Croatia's struggle to avert economic disaster by reconstructing itself in the image of the prosperous free-market economies of the West, together with her competing tendency to embrace an exclusivist-nationalist political rhetoric, continues to have significant, if uncertain, effects on the lives of Croatian Jews as well as ordinary non-Jewish Croatian citizens. The attempt to sort them out, particularly with respect to the future of the Zagrebian Jewish community, provides a critical point of departure for the ethnographic narrative that unfolds in the following chapters.

# Introduction

This book is about Jewish community life in postcommunist Croatia. Through ethnohistoric research in the ŽOZ, I explore the complex of strategies employed by Croatian Jews in refashioning the significance of their community in the postcommunist era. Tracing the community's turbulent history from its inception in the late eighteenth century to the Jewish community renewal movements that swept through east-central Europe from the mid-1980s through the 1990s, I discuss how Croatia's transition from Yugoslavia has impacted the lives of a small community of largely intercultural Jews. In doing so, I pay particular attention to the impact of local and transnational cultural shifts during this period, wherein Jewish community life in Croatia became the focus of a number of institutional forces, such as market capitalism, government-sponsored diversity campaigns, and transnational identity politics—forces that I refer to as the postcommunist "meaning makers" of the Jewish community. The narratives of ŽOZ members (collected between 1997–2000 and during shorter subsequent fieldtrips to Croatia between 2001–2004) are analyzed in terms of various forces that have reshaped the newer meanings of the Jewish community, including the collapse of communism, the influence of international Jewish support organizations, the rise of xenophobia, and the emergence of the Croatian nation-state in 1991.

Several important factors that characterize Croatian Jewry surfaced from the ethnohistoric approach employed in this study; in particular, the community's long-standing cultural integration trends and secular history rooted in the tenets of modernity, the development of urban centers in east-central Europe, the Jewish Enlightenment, as well as an abiding cosmopolitanism that managed to survive sixty years of communism into the postcommunist era. Cosmopolitanism—a concept that is entrenched in the birth of the nation-state some two centuries ago—is expressed in the postcommunist era through "feeling Jewish," that is, a sense of nostalgia about Jewish cultural and intel-

1

lectual history, and a shared identification as "citizens of the world."[1] The feeling of having "world citizenship" and interest in Jewish culture explains why Croatian Jews recognize the importance of Judaism to the sustenance of their community, even though most have had little or no exposure to Judaism and are generally not interested in the adoption of "traditional," or ghetto-ized, Jewish lifestyles. Croatian Jews, who identify as humanists and world citizens, view involvement in religious observance as backward, psychologi-cally demanding, and ultimately contrary to the humanistic and cosmopolitan values that have come to signify the history of the Jewish Croatian commu-nity.[2]

Although the community has witnessed a number of cycles of rapid social changes through its two-hundred-year existence, certain aspects that distin-guish Croatian Jews from neighboring Jewish communities remain unchanged. For example, Croatian Jews generally have not been ostracized from Croatian society. Unlike their brethren to the east and west (Italy), whose lives were either confined to the *shtetl*, or Jewish urban ghettos, Cro-atian Jews were integrated, emancipated, and upwardly mobile. This success-ful adaptation to the ambient culture and largely cosmopolitan identity raises a number of questions pertaining to the continuation of the Jewish commu-nity after World War II. How, for example, did Croatian Jews manage to uphold bonds of loyalty to their communities in light of cultural integration, secularization, and the experience of sixty years of communism? As the nar-ratives of my consultants imply, the central variable in the refashioning of the cultural community is the intercultural background of most Croatian Jews, which in turn raises questions concerning the conceptualization of the Jewish community that an anthropological analysis must address.[3] For example, how and why do individuals from intercultural backgrounds choose to identify as Jews? What other options do such individuals have in the post-communist era? Why have highly nostalgic meanings associated with cultural identifica-tion become desirable? How does the conceptualization of the community reflect the particular history of Croatian Jews, transnational identity politics, the xenophobic 1990s, and the collapse of communism?

In order to better situate these questions historically and ethnographically, I begin by describing the ways in which the changing sociopolitical landscape has impacted Croatian Jewry. The historic portion of my study (chapters 1 and 2) describes the cultural background in which the Jewish Croatian com-munity is located from the late eighteenth century (when Jews were allowed to reside in Croatia for up to three days for trading purposes) to the annihila-tion of the community during the Holocaust, its subsequent reemergence dur-ing Tito's Yugoslavia, and its continuation in the postcommunist era. The ethnographic portion of my study (chapters 3, 4, 5, and 6) focuses on the newer meanings of the Jewish community in light of the disintegration of Yugoslavia and the reemergence of an independent Croatia in 1991. The cultural underpinnings of the community space as a site in which the Jewish community is imagined and reproduced, and the arrival of a spiritual leader are issues that are explored through the narratives of ŽOZ members. Throughout, I focus on many ŽOZ members' interest in reconnecting with their Jewishness, their perceptions of the community rabbi, and their visions for the future of the community. In the last, ethnohistoric chapter (chapter 6), I examine the role of domestic and international support organizations in reshaping the meaning of Jewish community life in Croatia. By exploring the complex of strategies employed by Croatian Jews in refashioning and maintaining their communities, I challenge both the nostalgic image of a thriving presence of Jewish culture in Croatia as well as the (more prominent) view that Jewish communities in Croatia are on the brink of distinction. I suggest that this latter view—the "disappearance thesis"—is belied by the experiences of many Croatian Jews, who continue to derive meaning from Jewish community life, notwithstanding their evident cultural polarization and lack of religious commitment.

Throughout my study, I juxtapose the hybridized cultural community against the much-idealized view of culture and the nation-state as homogeneous. Rejecting essentialist views of cultural community, I suggest that cultural communities are in an ongoing process of reinvention, transformation, and renegotiation of the meanings that best fit their particular circumstances. Socialization and cultural heritage are not the only or the most legitimate forms of cultural identity construction; rather, these are two variables in a broader complex of negotiated cultural experiences. Observations that depict the dynamic nature of the cultural community continue to be valuable because they show that the construction of the cultural community is not rooted in essentialist paradigms, but is instead subject to ongoing cultural adjustments.

Employing cultural analysis—a framework which regards culture as mutable, emergent, and rooted in local and transnational political economies as well as enduring social relations—I address three themes that continue to characterize the Jewish Croatian community: cultural integration, hybridization, and the intercultural background of Croatian Jews. *Community* is analyzed in terms of its ideological meanings, as physical place in which social relations are reproduced, and as a way of differentiating insiders from outsiders. Cultural analysis provides a lens through which the normative context of everyday life experiences, social actions and perceptions of individuals can be examined. It begins with the premise that people's experiences, actions, and perceptions (ideologies) are culturally constituted. As such, it is concerned with understanding the *meanings* behind people's experiences and their beliefs. The things that people experience and believe reveal culturally constructed values, as well as the economic and political systems that underpin such values. Thus, from a cultural analysis perspective, *community* conveys a response to the cultural values and social practices that are embedded in a given time and place (locally, cross-culturally, or in a transnational context).

In light of the themes that continue to characterize the Jewish Croatian community (cultural integration, hybridization, and the intercultural marriage patterns of Croatian Jews), I turn now to a discussion of a number of ideas put forth by scholars writing about cultural communities in transition: the dichotomy of essentialism versus constructivism, the so-called Jewish identity crisis, and the cultural contexts in which the meaning making institutions that support the Jewish community can be understood.

## ESSENTIALISM VERSUS CONSTRUCTIVISM

One of the challenges of anthropological analysis is to transcend binary oppositions such as authentic/inauthentic or essentialist/antiessentialist constructions of culture. While an essentialist paradigm has long been criticized by social scientists, there is a sense in which it captures the way in which intercultural individuals negotiate their chosen community. To be sure, the cultural community holds primary meaning only in the context of people's experiences and the social politics of a given time and place. The struggle for the meaning of the Jewish community is further complicated by an individual's understanding of who an *echte* (real) or *authentic* Jew is. In its view of group membership as based on *consanguineal* ties, Jewish religious law is clear about who is considered Jewish and who is not. However, these ideas are not easily applied to a largely intercultural community of Jews.

According to Clifford Geertz (1973), an essentialist view of the cultural community regards features such as family, tradition, and heritage as fixed and unchanging, rather than constructed by social contingencies. On this view, the cultural community unifies group members by virtue of its seamless transmission through families, tradition, and heritage. For essentialists, a sensory experience, sometimes exemplified through the notion of "shared blood," lies at the heart of the cultural community, contributing to a sense of innate oneness and homogeneity experienced by group members. Essentialist views incorporate meanings associated with imaginary blood-ties among group members. Such views have the effect of strongly juxtaposing self from other, or the in-group from the out-group. For essentialists, the cultural community is understood through presumed personal characteristics that are inherited through a set of immutable customs and values. Notions of sameness (e.g., Jewish looks, the Jewish spirit, and Jewish predispositions) and otherness (e.g., non-Jewish looks, non-Jewish sensibilities, and so on) are emphasized.

Contrary to the essentialist view outlined above, constructivists maintain that cultural communities are imagined and continuously reshaped by the ambient sociocultural environment. Rather than being fixed or derived solely through birthright, constructivists regard the cultural community as a transformative community that is mediated by social relationships and subject to continual readjustment by its environment. According to this view, there is a continuum along which the cultural community exists in an ongoing process of negotiation—a process that is mediated by interaction with group members, outsiders, and national and international political economies. Constructivist views are rooted in humanist values of tolerance and liberal democracy. Yet, ultimately, constructivists view culture and identity as fictions that are contingent upon opportunity, serendipity, and the political reality of time, rather than imaginary blood-ties (Clifford and Marcus, 1986; Rosaldo, 1989; Rubin, 1975).

While constructivism provides a useful alternative to the rigidity of the essentialist view of the cultural community, it neither details the process of construction and transformation, nor explains how and why particular cultural meanings are ascribed to a *chosen* community.[4] Intercultural Jews in Croatia, for example, rely strongly on essentialist notions of identity construction in order to feel connected to their cultural communities. Not being able to trace their Jewish heritage back to their immediate families, or to the experience of Jewish cultural practices passed down from previous generations, intercultural Jews nevertheless cultivate a sense of homogeneity with others in order to overcome feelings of inadequacy and illegitimacy. This strategy becomes even more important for individuals who became vulnerable to discrimination during the transformation of the Yugoslav nation-state. Indeed, symbolic essentialism is often employed in order to justify one's membership in a chosen cultural community, particularly during periods of nationalism when minority cultures are made to feel like outsiders.[5] This strategy provides insights to the multiple and contextual meanings of identity that are highly applicable to intercultural Jews living in postcommunist states in transition.

## THE DISAPPEARANCE THESIS

Due to growing secularization and intermarriage among Jews in Europe and elsewhere, a number of scholars, community organizers, and Jewish support organizations have predicted the disappearance of the Jewish community. According to this "disappearance thesis," the encroachment of secularism will eventually dissolve all religious communities. Concerned with the future of Jewry around the globe, scholars have articulated the so-called *silent Holocaust*, or the *crisis of Jewish identity*.

The view that a decline in Jewish religiosity will eventually result in a weaker sense of Jewish identity or, in the extreme, the disintegration of the Jewish community, has been suggested by a number of scholars who have studied Jews in the United States (Amyot and Singelman 1996; Bakalian, 1993; Cohen, 1983). A similar view has been advanced by scholars studying Jews in Europe (DellaPergola, 1994; Gordiejew, 1999; Schweid, 1994) and is epitomized by Harriet Pass Freidenreich's remark that "the vibrant Jewish communities of interwar Yugoslavia, well adapted to survival in a multinational state, live on today as memories, not as realities" (Freidenreich 1984:210). Scholars writing about the dangers of intermarriage have also suggested this view (Borneman and Peck, 1995).

Proponents of the disappearance thesis argue that the predominately secular and intercultural background of Croatian Jews creates a crisis for Jewish identity in the sense that Croatian Jews are viewed neither as Croats (an ethnic/religious designation) nor as *authentic* Jews by Jewish religious law. Life under communism, along with the diminishing number of Jews living in Croatia after World War II (in which 80 percent of the community perished), and the correspondingly high rates of intercultural marriages are often cited as the central causes of this putative crisis.

To undo the alleged crisis requires rescuing Jews from the evils of communism and rehabilitating them into Jews for whom religious observance and marriage to bona fide Jews are matters of importance. The proponents of the disappearance thesis have argued this point, thereby encouraging Jewish community renewal movements in the mid-1980s through the 1990s. During this period, many believed that the only way out of the so-called crisis was through conversion and religious observance. Jewish philanthropic organizations active in east-central Europe called for a return to "traditional" Jewish values. Guided by their convictions, these organizations tended to view the secular nature of postcommunist Jewish community life as a threat to the very existence of Jewish identity (Weiner, 2003). In light of this, Jewish community centers throughout east-central Europe have received generous financial support from international Jewish organizations. Some of this support has been earmarked for cultural programs designed to promote a traditional version of the Jewish community.

In the end, the attention bestowed on Jewish communities in east-central Europe, along with the rapid cultural changes that Croatia experienced in the 1990s, has significantly influenced the self-perception of the Jewish Croatian community. Human rights issues and the treatment of minority cultures have become important topics of debate in Croatia's postcommunist era, particularly in light of frequent public expressions of anti-Semitism, racism, or discrimination. Interestingly, the proponents of the disappearance thesis have argued that a decline in discrimination against Jews will produce a corresponding decline in Jewish community life (Eisen, 1994; Horowitz, 1985; Keller, 1966). Others maintain that exclusivist nationalism reverses this process (Bowman, 1994; Brass, 1991; Connor, 1994; Denitch, 1994). The dissolution of Tito's Yugoslavia is an apt example. Contrary to the prediction that all cultural groups would eventually dissolve and, through Tito's self-managing socialism, fuse into a homogeneous social unit, the consciousness of cultural communities has been on the rise in Croatia since the late 1960s. Over the course of this process, Jewish community life has been negotiated in relation to the ambient (local and community-based) political climate and in response to the pressures of communism, the xenophobia of the Tuđman era, and the community revival objectives of international support organizations. And contrary to the premise of the disappearance thesis, my ethnohistoric analysis of the Jewish Croatian community reveals the Jewish community has been a site for predominately secular interpretations of Jewish identity since its inception. Moreover, my research indicates that since the 1990s, the exclusion from an *authentic* Croatian identity has made Jewish cultural identity even more appealing.

## CULTURAL COMMUNITY REVIVAL AND MEANING-MAKING INSTITUTIONS

In Zagreb, where most Croatian Jews live, membership in the *općina* experienced a 14 percent rise in the years prior to and following the emergence of the Croatian nation-state. One factor that is directly associated with the increase in membership is changes in the rules for membership implemented by Slavko Goldstein, the last president of the ŽOZ in the former Yugoslavia from 1986–1990. Goldstein's reforms granted ŽOZ community affiliation to non-Jewish spouses as well as persons able to trace their Jewish ancestry back to a grandparent. Goldstein believed that the descendents of people who had risked persecution under the racial laws of the 1930s should be allowed membership, if only as a way of ensuring a safe haven in a time of future crisis. He employed criteria similar to those described in Israel's *Law of Return* policy, which provides the right of repatriation to all Jews and family members of two descending generations. Regardless of membership reform, a number of intercultural Jews who returned to the ŽOZ community during the 1990s arguably did so because of the experience of loss and identity crisis during Croatia's transition from Yugoslavia. These events are described more fully in chapters 2 and 3.

Other factors that led to the reconceptualization of the Jewish community and the increase in ŽOZ membership can be traced to the newer meanings of the cultural community. Voluntary in association and expression, the historically hybridized Jewish community mobilized its members through participation in a variety of social activities that were ultimately made meaningful in relation to, and through interaction with, fellow community members (Barth, 1979; Eriksen, 1993). In light of this, there is a continuum along which the construction of the cultural community is made visible and meaningful vis-à-vis "cultural others," as well as community members.

Thoroughly contextual and closely related to the idea of distinction is the notion that the cultural community produces feelings of cohesion and solidarity through its assertion of difference. As Gregory Bateson (1979) puts it, "It takes two [communities] to create a difference—each alone is a non-entity, a non-being." Such feelings of distinction are further emphasized during times of sociopolitical upheaval. For European Jews, the symbols of distinction are deeply rooted in the experience of a long history of persecution and the Holocaust, along with the void of such memories often experienced by second generation Holocaust survivors.

Notwithstanding the history of the Jews, memories, or the absence of memory, Croatian Jews have additional shared experiences of cultural hybridization, cosmopolitanism, and high intercultural marriage patterns that distinguish them from non-Jewish Croatians. These experiences reach back to the beginnings of the Jewish settlements (approximately two hundred years ago) in the Croatian region. The assertion of symbols of distinction through religious artifacts, food, festivals, and other social activities has become an important vehicle for expressing and celebrating Jewish cultural identity. Moreover, Jewish education and an engagement with Jewish heritage place community values into a new, consumerist-oriented and identity politics-driven system of meanings. The boundaries of such a system (where "one of us" ends and otherness begins) serve to unite the community around a common set of ideas, in which the cultural community functions primarily as a site of social interaction and nostalgic reckoning of "community" and "identity." These newer meanings of the cultural community, experienced through the foregoing meaning-making symbols, are fueled by transnational identity politics and encoded in material (e.g., the organization of the physical space of the ŽOZ) and emotional (e.g., the maintenance of social friendship networks and various other types of social interaction) ties.

Looking beyond the physical community space of the ŽOZ, which functions as a conduit for identity expression, a cultural analysis of the social organization of the space provides useful insights into Croatia's changing political economy, particularly its transition from communism to capitalism. Examining the material reality of the cultural community through the social organization of the ŽOZ, as well as through the narratives of consultants, a clearer picture emerges—one that reveals a system of meaning rooted in Croatia's desire to disassociate itself with communism and to acquire membership in the European Union. Croatia's endorsement of cultural diversity is designed to appease the European Union. One example of this is Croatia's promotion of the Jewish community through cultural diversity programs sponsored by the Croatian Ministry of Culture. However, these programs, premised on the view that all cultural "others" must be submerged in tradition and religion, conflict with the self-image of many Croatian Jews. The conflict is analogous in some ways to the tension created by the efforts of international Jewish organizations in promoting the Jewish community by emphasizing the importance of religious consciousness. In their attempt to undo the Jewish identity crisis, such organizations seek to cultivate Jewish religiosity and promote a separatist Jewish identity.

## FIELDWORK

My fieldwork was conducted in several stages. In order to write my dissertation, I visited the community over the course of three consecutive trips to Croatia between 1997 and 2000. Subsequent shorter fieldwork trips brought me back to Croatia in 2001, 2003, and finally in 2004. Most of the data collected for chapters 3 and 4 was collected since 2000. During my initial visits, I relied mostly on participant observation and informal interviews with non-Jewish and Jewish Croatians. I kept abreast of local political events via the news media and by attending lectures at the Europa House, as well as at Zagreb University, and Dubrovnik, a south Croatian coastal town. Prior to Tuđman's death in 2000, Croatia was in political turmoil. During this time, the news media focused on social, cultural and economic issues related to the transition and Tuđman's government. I discussed many of these issues with my consultants. These conversations were usually combined into discussions about the *općina*. But there was another reason for discussing Croatian politics. Almost everyone I spoke with was eager to express his or her views on national politics and understood the social issues associated with Croatia's transition from Yugoslavia as having a direct impact on their lives. Because of that, I was able to learn more about the lives of my consultants outside the context of the *općina*. Six years after the initial stupor phase following the formation of the Croatian state, feelings of emptiness, loss, and disillusionment were widespread. By 1997 consultants had either gotten over mourning the loss of Yugoslavia or they continued to harbor nostalgic ideas about Yugoslavism—an ideology that, along with many Croats, they had wholeheartedly embraced for much of their lives.

I attended biweekly lectures held at the ŽOZ and participated in most other social activities offered by the ŽOZ, including Friday night services, a weekly Torah study group, ceramics, folklore dance workshops, senior and youth group meetings; monthly Family Sabbath gatherings and Jewish women's meetings; and bimonthly seminars on Jewish education. In addition to these social activities, I was invited to teach an English conversation course, which met weekly for four months.

I am indebted to my English language students who shared their wisdom, joy, and above all, their laughter with me. The conversation class became a ritual, and like all rituals, it was divided into a sequence of events, including casual conversation before class (in Croatian), class discussion, and the obligatory *kaffeeklatsch* in the elegant *klub* after class. My students—most of them retired and of few means—collected money and bought me a diamond ring for my birthday. Leona, an elderly woman who had survived the horrors of the Holocaust in neighboring Hungary, baked a birthday cake for the occasion in the shape of a heart with little legs attached to it. She said, "You are a big heart with legs." Much of my popularity in the class, I believe, was due to the fact that I encouraged my students to express themselves through the class, a rather novel concept for most. The articles that we read together were about "things Jewish," and students were asked to tell about the first time they came to the *općina*. The class had a dual function for me: it allowed me to get to know the community members better (which gave me an opportunity to be introduced to potential interviewees), and it also enabled me to give something back to the community even though, in the end, I was the one that got the most out of the experience. It was in class that I met my "field mother."

Apart from an array of ŽOZ social activities, I also participated in a number of events pertinent to Jewish and Croatian culture. As is common among those who employ an ethnographic approach, I set out to immerse myself in Croatian culture and attended as many events as I could. Among these were the May 9 antifascist demonstration on the Victims of Fascism Square, the

May 5 Woman's Day gathering at the Slovenia House, Holocaust Remembrance Day at the Jewish cemetery in Zagreb, and the Minority Celebration Festival in Zagreb's Lisinski Hall. I also paid a short visit to a number of smaller Jewish communities in Split, Dubrovnik, and Ljubljana (in Slovenia), followed by two short trips to Hungary—one with a youth group and another with an older group of Jewish Croatians. The youth gathering in Hungary was organized by members of Jewish communities dispersed throughout the former Yugoslavia, including Jews from Sarajevo (Bosnia), Belgrade (Serbia), and Ljubljana (Slovenia). Although these meetings were mostly social, some people from the *općina* noted that the excursions provided an opportunity to meet other Jews and potential marriage partners. Although no marriages or romantic liaisons resulted from these trips, to my knowledge, many friendships were initiated during summer camp excursions on the Adriatic coast. My second trip to Hungary was with older Croatian Jews. Here, again, the meetings brought together members of different Jewish communities throughout the former Yugoslavia and were predominantly for the purpose of maintaining long-standing friendship networks. Much of the gathering was centered on conversation and food, and the highlight of the event was the Friday night dinner.

Apart from the lighting of Sabbath candles, there was little to distinguish these dinners from any non-Jewish social gathering. After my excursions to Hungary, others events were organized. These events were somewhat more educational, focusing on Jewish cultural heritage. Beginning in the summer of 2000, and in the years that followed, a weeklong event was organized which focused on Jewish education, history, food preparation, music, and spirituality. The demand for these events reflects the newer meanings of the Jewish community and the 1998 arrival of the first full-time rabbi in Croatia since 1943.

Although I established intense connections with a number of consultants, I choose to employ the collective narrative form because I want to focus on the reconstruction of the cultural community. Differently put, the ethnographic descriptions of this study are not traced through the lives of key consultants—as has become the convention in ethnographic writing—but instead through a collection of verbatim statements or vignettes for the purpose of illustrating certain points. That said, I worked closely with two key consultants throughout my research: an observant member who introduced me to the spiritual world in the ŽOZ, and his antagonist, who defined herself as a secular Jew. Both were invaluable resources. They respected my position in the *općina* as well as my social engagement in both religious and cultural activities—although neither would have participated in both spheres of activity. I took many of their views to be representative of the religious minority in the community, and of the majority of Croatian Jews who identify as secular, humanistic, or cultural Jews.

In order to preserve anonymity, I have changed the names of all my consultants (except for public figures in the community), and on different occasions, I have changed their gender and, when appropriate, their ages. I have also created pseudoidentities by splicing together individual narratives that are representative of particular issues. In light of these precautions, consultants were also informed that the information they provided would be kept in strict confidence and that individuals would not be exposed as a result of their participation. During the second phase of my study (after 2000), I obtained Institutional Review Board (IRB) approval in order to further protect the confidentiality of the consultants. Consultants were informed prior to the interviews that they could withdraw from the study at any point or choose not to answer any of my questions.

Most of my interviews took place in the ŽOZ. I also met people in cafés or restaurants in downtown Zagreb and in the smaller communities that I visited. I conducted interviews with a total of forty individuals—slightly more women than men (twenty-four to sixteen), with consultants ranging in age from nineteen to eighty-seven. Most of my interviewees had received higher education. Some were retired, some were students, but most were working professionals. The interviews took anywhere from one to three hours, and many conversations extended far beyond the questions I had prepared. The bulk of the interviews conducted in 2003 were audiotaped, transcribed, and translated from Croatian to English. The initial 1999 interviews were not taped. During those, I mostly took notes in English, but included sentences or unknown words in Croatian, which I would either look up after the interview or ask about during subsequent conversations.

For reference material, I relied chiefly on secondary texts. The libraries at the Ethnographic Institute, the ŽOZ, the Ethnology Department at Zagreb University, Purdue University in West Lafayette, Indiana, and DePaul University in Chicago, Illinois, were made available to me. The historical information for chapter 2 was drawn from texts acquired from the national library in Zagreb and through interlibrary loans from the United States, as well as through oral histories collected during my interviews. Newspaper articles and the Internet provided additional valuable sources of information. I was able to keep in touch with several consultants by e-mail and through conventional correspondence during the time I was writing at Purdue University and later, while employed as an Assistant Professor at DePaul University. At DePaul, I obtained research assistance formally, through grants, and informally, through interested native-speaking students. Their help proved to be invaluable. I also had the opportunity to work with research assistants in Croatia, who transcribed and translated the taped interviews.

## ORGANIZATION OF THE CHAPTERS

One of the central goals of this study is to achieve a deeper understanding of how cultural communities reflect the shifting sociopolitical climates in which they are situated. I approach this task by locating the Jewish community within the local (national and community-based) political economy, transnational identity politics, and the historical situatedness of the Croatian Jews. Chapters 1 and 2 convey historic information; chapters 3, 4, and 5 are largely ethnographic; and chapter 6 employs an ethnohistoric symbiosis.

In chapter 1, I develop the sociopolitical backdrop against which I interpret the experiences of Croatian Jews. Three salient periods in the history of Croatian Jews are addressed: Jewish life in the nineteenth century, the pre–World War II development of Jewish societies and associations, and the post-Holocaust period from 1945 to the mid-1980s. The stories and the history of the Jewish community in Zagreb provide a context for posing several key questions regarding identity. These questions range from the changing meaning of Jewish community life in Croatia and what remains of Jewish community life as it once existed, to how developments such as modernization, industrialization, and the disintegration of the Austro-Hungarian empire have affected the meaning of community for Jews. In exploring these questions, I show that Jewish secular identities, rather than marking the disappearance of Croatian Jews, have long been relatively permanent features of Jewish community life in Croatia.

Chapter 2 explores the conceptualization of Jewish identity during the former Yugoslavia through the 1990s. Here, I focus on a number of key phenomena, including the self-managing socialism of Tito's Yugoslavia; the Croatian separatist movements of the 1970s and 1990s; the rise of xenophobia in the 1990s; and the Croatian government's treatment of Jews living within its borders. Data taken from national census surveys suggest that the Croatian separatist movement of the 1970s did not have as dramatic an impact on Croatian Jews as the more recent 1990s resurgence of Croatian nationalism, which ostracized Croatian Jews and some other minority groups by labeling them as outsiders. In light of the foregoing, I discuss how communism and recent Croatian sociopolitical reforms have influenced the lives of Croatian Jews, and how the construction of Jews as *outsiders* has made affiliation with the ŽOZ a desirable choice for many intercultural Croatian Jews.

In chapter 3, I address the social organization of the ŽOZ and the post-communist meaning of Jewish identity. In ,doing so, I extend the ideas discussed in previous chapters by arguing that the social trends that characterized Jewish community life in the nineteenth century persisted throughout the twentieth century. In particular, stories about the ŽOZ indicate that Jewish community life continues to be defined in terms of social friendship networks and various types of cultural and political.affiliations. Many of these stories reveal that the ŽOZ continues to function as the primary location in which Jewish community life is experienced, contested, and enacted. Examining them, I raise questions regarding the different expressions of Jewish identity in the community and the role of the ŽOZ in facilitating them. Extending the historical context of the ŽOZ to the sphere of social interaction, I argue that the community space, in which Jewish identities are continually reshaped, is used ultimately for the purpose of expressing Jewish culture.

Chapter 4 explores the competing views of the meaning of the ŽOZ community. Through the narratives of ŽOZ members, I address two interrelated themes: the arrival of the community rabbi in 1998 and the conceptualization of the *Praška* space. The 1998 arrival of the community rabbi was a watershed event in the ŽOZ's history, which produced tension between Jewish religious laws and the diverse and sometimes competing expressions of Jewish identity within the community. Now an empty lot, the *Praška* space marks the former site of Zagreb's only synagogue (destroyed in 1941) and the potential future site of the *općina*. I employ these themes as a lens through which to explore the conflict between traditionalist and the integrationalist or humanist understanding of the ŽOZ. In doing so, I examine the direction of the spiritual leadership of the ŽOZ and the debates over the form, function and future of the ŽOZ.

In chapter 5, I discuss how and why intercultural Jews choose to identify as Jews. In particular, I explore the interest shared by many ŽOZ members in connecting with their cultural heritage and with the newer meanings of Jewish identity. To do so, I consider several factors that presuppose the meaning of Jewish identity and point out that, for many intercultural Jews, the process of identity negotiation is dependent upon symbolic essentialism. As the narratives of the ŽOZ members reveal, Jewish identity is contingent throughout an individual's lifetime and is therefore continually subject to external (social and political) as well as internal (emotional) change.

In chapter 6, I examine the Jewish community's relationship to national politics—particularly Croatia's interest in European Union membership—as well as to external, and often highly politicized, processes that threaten to determine the meaning of Jewish identity. I pay particular attention to the role of local Croatian cultural diversity programs and international Jewish support organizations in shaping Jewish community life in Croatia. I argue that these roles are related by a similar vision of Jewishness that is in conflict with the identities of the ŽOZ members themselves.

In the conclusion, I situate the meanings of the Jewish Croatian community within a broader theoretical framework. I begin this task by revisiting the theoretical underpinnings of the construction of the ŽOZ, as set forth in this introduction and developed in subsequent chapters. Along the way, I reaffirm the bases of my critique of the disappearance thesis, and its inability to explain the lived experiences of Croatian Jews. In short, I suggest that what is needed in order to make sense of the intercultural experiences of Jews living in contemporary Croatian society is a more thorough look at their historical situatedness, both in terms of the ambient political environment, and the transnational identity politics that influence the present and future of the ŽOZ community.

## NOTES

1. The acculturated (or culturally integrated) status of Croatian Jews relates to their adaptation to a new social and cultural environment (along with the local cultural norms)—a social phenomenon which did not necessarily lead to the loss of cultural distinction, but which marked Jewish community life within the Austro-Hungarian Empire in the eighteenth and nineteenth centuries. Nineteenth-century Croatian Jews were acculturated in the sense that they did not speak Yiddish or Ladino; they did not live in separate neighborhoods; and social interaction with fellow Jews was a matter of individual preference, not communal obligations.

2. Similar to ideas about religiosity are perceptions about Jewish ethnicity. *Ethnicity* is not a desirable term for describing Jewish Croatian self-identity because it carries negative connotations associated with "ethnic cleansing" and "ethnic separatism," which are in turn associated with a departure from Tito's self-managing socialism.

3. There are several different ways in which the cultural community can be understood. The formation of various cultural societies and other voluntary associations is not a modern phenomenon. Ferdinant Tönnies ([1887] 1963) described *gesellschaft* as the cultural community that replaced the "traditional community," which he viewed as rooted in primary relationships that were found rather than made. For Tönnies, the distinguishing feature of a *gesellschaft* community is expressed in individualism, sentimentality, and loyalty. In such a community, social relations are formalized and developed later in life— they are maintained through the negotiation of personal interests rather than obligations.

4. I borrow the term *chosen community* from Kath Weston (1991), who argues that kinship and other communities are fictional and traceable to cultural norms.

5. The term I employ is inspired by Herbert Gans's symbolic ethnicity and symbolic religiosity. Gans (1994) uses the related concepts of symbolic ethnicity and symbolic religiosity to refer to a range of strategies associated with ethnic and religious identity negotiation in contemporary societies. Symbolic ethnicity helps to mitigate the social and

psychological upheaval experienced by cultural groups as they adapt to a postmodern world, in which interaction associated with mono-locality is disappearing. Gans argues that this explains why ethnic cultures do not experience the straight-line assimilation patterns that melting-pot theorists have proposed, but instead respond to social pressures with patterns of behavior in which ethnic and religious identities are maintained on an idiosyncratic basis. His model of symbolic ethnicity appropriately describes the importance of nostalgia to the negotiation of the cultural community. A concern with Jewish identity rooted in nostalgia and sentiment ("cultural Judaism") as opposed to rigorous adherence to Judaic practices and "traditions" is paradigmatic of symbolic ethnicity.

*Chapter One*

# Tracing the Meaning of Two Hundred Years of Jewish Community Life

At the start of World War II, approximately 23,000 Jews lived in what currently constitutes Croatia. Close to 11,000, (90 percent, of the permanent Jewish population in Croatia at that time), were residents of Zagreb and about 12,000 were refugees from Nazi-occupied areas throughout Europe. The majority of the Zagreb Jews were Ashkenazi and identified as *Neologue* observers, and about 600 individuals, dispersed throughout Croatia but predominantly from Zagreb, were Sephardic.[1] An even smaller number of Croatian Jewry (about 140 individuals) where identified as Orthodox observers who maintained separate lifestyles. Those proportions remained remarkably similar at the turn of the new millennium, long after the Jewish community had been diminished during the Holocaust. Following the atrocities of the Holocaust, about 2,500 Croatian Jews belonging to nine Jewish community centers constituted the country's smallest cultural minority. At present, the most vibrant community remains in Zagreb, where about 2,000 individuals reside, of whom 1,500 claim membership in the ŽOZ—a number that has risen significantly during the last decade.[2] The other communities have less than 50 members each.

The story of Croatian Jewry is told through the story of the Jews of Zagreb, both because of the proportionally large number of Croatian Jews in Zagreb and the vibrant cultural activity there. Zagrebian Jews, and Croatian Jews more generally, were relatively recent immigrants to the Croatian region in the last quarter of the eighteenth century, at the time a province of the Austro-Hungarian empire. Those Jews who lived in the Empire enjoyed civil liberties not granted to Jews living to the east, in present-day Russia and Poland. This meant that the differences in lifestyle and worldview between east-central European Jews and Jews living in places such as Vienna, Budapest, and

Zagreb began to increase. Croatian Jews living in urban areas (where most European Jews lived) had more opportunities for education, entrepreneurship, and upward mobility than *shtetl*-dwellers, and this relatively favorable social status is reflected in their linguistic and cultural traditions.

Jewish participation in civil life, and the corresponding opportunities to become upwardly mobile, backfired in the twentieth century when anti-Semitism regained its popularity in many European nations and Jewish cosmopolitanism became equated with the "international proletarian lobby." Well before the Holocaust, European Jews responded in a number of different ways to the threat of having their civil and human rights compromised. Zionism, popularized by the writings of Theodor Hertzl and Mosses Hess (1820–1875), was perhaps the most important and lasting response. Although few individuals planned to actually immigrate to the Jewish homeland before the Holocaust, Zionism and the growing emphasis on Jewish nationhood had a powerful influence on Jewish community life in the early twentieth century (Freidenreich, 1984; Gordiejew, 1999; Hayden, 1992; Webber, 1994). For those who were strongly committed to the establishment of a Jewish nation-state, this meant a sense of solidarity articulated through membership in a number of local socialist-oriented Jewish organizations. It also meant that for the first time Jews were able to assert their cultural identities outside of a religious or "traditional" context. Zionism provided an ideal way for emancipated Jews to identify with a secular sociopolitical movement without severing their ties with the Jewish world and their communities. Jewish identities articulated at that time emulated Jewish Enlightenment thinking. They also reflected the short-lived success of Jews in Croatian civil life.

Other responses to the rise of national sovereignty movements within the Empire included radical assimilation and—echoing Jews living in the East—Orthodox separatism. Neither response was widespread; however, a small but vibrant contingent of Orthodox Jewry disassociated themselves from the growing integrated Jewish community. Another response to the increasing xenophobia was the rise of non-Jewish marriages that promised, but did not always deliver, increased civil rights, along with social and political mobility. Intercultural marriage rates would rise again in the 1950s, a time when few marriageable Jewish partners remained. Intercultural marriages and the production of multiple cultural heritages would eventually make Jewish cultural identity an attractive option during the community's renaissance in the 1980s—a trend that the grandparents or parents of intercultural individuals would have looked upon disdainfully.

In order to understand the development of these responses and situate Croatian Jews in their current social and cultural environment, I offer a brief account of three salient periods of Jewish community life in Croatia: the period from the late eighteenth century through the early twentieth century; the pre–World War II era of development of Jewish organizations and associations; the years of the Holocaust and the post war reestablishment of the Jewish community. Beginning with an overview of Jewish community life in Zagreb in the nineteenth century, I focus on the contribution of Jews in the context of the Zagreb's merchant history. In particular, I argue that the expansion and economic development of Zagreb, together with the opportunity for Jews to become upwardly mobile, played a significant role in the development of Jewish social and cultural organizations, and the community's desire to become integrated into the local environment. Next, I argue that the arrival of Jewish organizations in the early part of the twentieth century forever transformed the meaning of Jewish community. In the final sections of the chapter, I examine the fate of the Croatian Jewish community during and after World War II.

The conceptualization and function of the Jewish community in each of these periods are addressed by employing historic accounts. The history of the Jewish community in Croatia—Zagreb in particular—provides a context for understanding how an increase in intercultural marriages and cultural integration, the modernization of Judaism, the establishment of Jewish social organizations in light of civil rights, and the growth of the urban metropolis have affected Croatian Jews. In exploring these questions, I show that Jewish secular identity, rather than the disappearance of Croatian Jews, has long been a relatively permanent feature of Jewish community life in Croatia.

## THE BEGINNINGS OF THE JEWISH COMMUNITY

The story of Croatian Jews begins in 1783, when an Edict of Tolerance was passed that allowed Jewish merchants to settle in present-day Zagreb. Zagreb, the most important colony for Jewish merchants in Croatia, became commercially successful due to its proximity to the Sava River. The city is predated by two settlements: Kaptol, which today is the seat of the Archbishop of Zagreb and the imposing Zagreb Cathedral, and Gradec, an important center of commerce in the region, dating back to the eleventh century.

Prior to the development of Zagreb in 1850, Kaptol and Gradec where ruled by several different empires, including the Hapsburg and Austro-Hungarian empires. During Hapsburg rule in the sixteenth century, heavy taxes were imposed on Gradec by Count Ulrich, the commander in chief of the region. Ulrich annulled all liberties of non-Catholics related to commerce and residence—a decision that forced the few Jews living in Gradec to leave.

Court files dating back to the sixteenth century indicate that the *Domus Judaeorum* (either a synagogue or some type of communal space) was evacuated (Bedenko, 1998). Gradec Jews returned centuries later when more sympathetic authorities passed new laws regarding the presence and settlement of foreign merchants.

After a series of invasions by the Ottoman Turks, Gradec tried reviving commerce by granting privileges to merchants and craftspeople. The Gradec market had become increasingly important for traveling merchants in the region. There is evidence dating back to the late 1700s of traveling Jewish salesmen, who were allowed to remain in the northern part of Croatia for up to three days (Freidenreich, 1984). As commerce grew, the towns expanded and special craft guilds emerged. The guilds functioned as exclusive associations where craftspeople of various trades could be affirmed, a cultural trend that in time would be reproduced in the twentieth century in the form of Jewish voluntary social organizations. Gradec's trade regulations, which were heavily monitored by the feudal system and controlled by the church authorities, restricted nonresidents from selling their merchandise in town.

In the mid-eighteenth century, the three-day trading arrangement in the northern part of Croatia changed. High-ranking officials from various smaller towns in the northwestern parts of Croatia endorsed the settlement of Jewish merchants in the region. Joseph II, the Emperor of the Hapsburg monarchy, passed an Edict of Tolerance (1783) that allowed Jews to settle in Gradec. Jews who settled in Gradec were merchants from regions within the Austro-Hungarian empire who spoke either Hungarian or German. In addition to the freedom of residence, the new arrivals were granted freedom of religious practice in exchange for a tax payment. The edict was essentially driven by economic motives. Joseph's advisors were under the impression that Jewish trade would bring prosperity to the region, as had been the case in the northern parts of Croatia. Indeed, when the second generation of Jewish merchants became successful some sixty years later, the tax laws were lifted. Although Jews were able to reside and practice their religion in Gradec, they were not able to choose their profession.

At the beginning of the nineteenth century, the Jewish community was still insignificant. It comprised only twenty families who lived in Gradec and the surrounding boroughs. Most Gradec Jews from other regions in the Austro-Hungarian empire spoke either Hungarian or German when they arrived. As the community grew, Jewish places of worship, schools, and organizations emerged. Restrictions on professions were lifted and jobs such as money changing were replaced by banking and financial advising. Animated by the desire to participate in Croatian civil society, Jews found opportunities in banking, commerce, the arts, medicine, and intellectual scholarship (Szabo, 1998). They became prominent residents of Zagreb. Croatian Jews were in fact more successful than Jews living in other areas throughout the former Yugoslavia. Their upward mobility and integration in civil society was reflected in the introduction of Croatian language instruction in Jewish schools and in the synagogue.

In the first part of the nineteenth century, Josip Jelačić, a colonel from the military frontier zone, was appointed to the position of Ban—the official in charge of internal administration, jurisprudence, religion and education. During his tenure, Jelačić brought about the separation of the church from civil authorities. As a result, the outdated feudal system was abolished and the first chamber of commerce and banking was established. Subsequent to these changes was the introduction of steamships on the Sava River, which made commercial life in the capital even more attractive. Croatian Jews, who played an important role in advancing Zagreb as a commercial center, began appearing as prominent citizens. For example, the first Jew was elected to city council in 1850. Many others, such as former merchants, became successful in banking and large-scale commerce.

Although their acculturated social status persists to the present day, the integration of Jews in pre-Holocaust Croatian civil society was short-lived. Their relative success began to crumble much earlier as Croats began questioning the Jews' loyalty to the Empire. In order to boost Croatian national consciousness, Croats used linguistic tools. Ljudevit Gaj, leading the first major nationalist movement in Croatia, founded several cultural organizations that used what later became standard Serbo-Croatian language in the first quarter of the nineteenth century when Croatian public life was dominated by the Magyar (Hungarian) language (Gazi, 1993). Employing the Croatian language as a unification tool, Gaj advocated the Illyrian project, which long after his death resulted in the independent Kingdom of Croatia in 1918.

The rise of Croatian, and later South Slav, nationalism, which tended to view Jews and those who did not speak Serbo-Croatian as *outsiders*, contributed to the Jews' linguistic and cultural acculturation. Croatian Jews who had arrived from regions within the Austro-Hungarian Empire spoke either Hungarian or German. These languages were not particularly desirable during Croatia's national awakening. As a result, Croatian Jews learned and taught Serbo-Croatian, and nearly 75 percent reported it as their native tongue by 1930 (Freidenreich, 1984). Some had Croaticized their personal and family names in an attempt to gain acceptance in Croatian society. As the Croatian economy began to flourish, great cultural differences were felt between rural Croatian peasants and the cosmopolitan urban culture of Zagreb, to which a professional class of Jews belonged. Most Croatian Jews had already adopted the ideals of modernity transferred through the *Haskalah*, or Jewish Enlightenment, out of which the *Neologue* movement had grown, while the peasant masses had not. As intensive industrial production began to sweep through Europe, an acceleration of growth in urban settlements occurred together with the "pariah status" bestowed upon the new urban, professional classes. Zagreb experienced rapid population growth from the late nineteenth to the early twentieth centuries (growing from 30,000 to 185,000), and an even greater boom after 1918 (Freidenreich, 1984). The Jewish population grew from 1,285 in 1880, to 8,702 in 1931 (I. Goldstein, 1998). The newly arrived peasant population lived mostly in the southwestern part of the town, which to this day remains a working-class neighborhood. The peasants who made the transition to a class of industrial workers experienced much hardship. Working conditions were not always favorable and the pay was often too low to make ends meet.

In contrast, the predominantly middle class Jewish population, never comprising more than 5 percent of the city's population, was doing well. Jews had not migrated to Zagreb as agricultural laborers but as merchants and salesmen who rapidly became upwardly mobile. Second and third generation Jews were able to study at the university and enjoy a relatively stable economy. Others, like the newer influx of small merchants who migrated from other towns throughout Croatia, worked in commerce, a profession that placed them socially well above industrial jobs and other forms of hard manual labor. In fact, more than 50 percent of the Jews throughout Croatia were involved in some type of commerce around the turn of the century (Szabo, 1998). The small merchants strongly identified as Zionists, embracing the socialist views of its visionaries.

This was also the time of Gaj's Illyrian project and South Slav nationalism, which eventually resulted in the independent Kingdom of Croatia in 1918. The Illyrian project was conceived on social ideals that were later interpreted as elitist. One response to the centralist forces that ruled the Kingdom of Yugoslavia was the emergence of the Croatian Communist Party that enjoyed short-lived success in the 1920s. Many among the growing professional class of Jews were in support of free-market political economies and, by extension, the kingdom. However, the Communist Party had some support from small Jewish merchants. The Communist Party achieved victory in Zagreb during the city council elections in 1920, when it won 39 percent of the votes, but soon after this triumph, all communist activities were banned (Kampus and Karaman, 1995).

Even though the communist workers movement was at its peak in Croatia in the 1920s, Nazi propaganda was not ignored. As Nazi doctrine swept throughout Europe, the Communist Party called for the organization of the national front against fascist invasions. Their efforts were put to a halt when a new government was formed in 1939 that gave in to German pressures and, a year later, built the first concentration camp in Yugoslavia at Bileće. The camp interned communists and those accused of opposing the regime. It was closed after only several months of operation due to strong protest from the public, an indication perhaps of the antifascist view shared by many Yugoslavs (S. Goldstein, 1998). Although fascism was essentially imported to Croatia, Croatian national separatists, led by Ante Pavelić, readily adopted its racist ideas.[3] Several laws were passed in the late 1930s, signaling the erosion of Jewish emancipation. By 1940, the employment of Jews in service of the state and in the education system was restricted (Švob, 1997). Jews were banned from engaging in the wholesale food business and were subjected to a limiting quota of Jewish enrollment at high schools and universities. In retrospect, these discriminatory regulations were mild in comparison to the atrocities committed by the *Ustaša* government that came to power in April 1941.

## THE DEVELOPMENT OF
## JEWISH ORGANIZATIONS

Changes in Croatia's urban demographics in the mid-nineteenth century resulted in the rapid reorganization of social life. A number of social and professional organizations emerged in Zagreb around 1850–1870. These included sports clubs and choirs that produced Croatian national songs, mountaineering organizations (whose activities began in the Zagrebačka Gora mountain range to the north of the city), and Croatian teaching and writers' associations. Although a growing number of Jews had become upwardly mobile, their participation in Croatian civil life remained limited. In order to compensate for this, various Jewish organizations devoted to social advancement, politics, and welfare emerged. Wealthy Jews, who supported the social needs of the poor, the elderly, and those unable to work, typically established these organizations. However tight-knit the Jewish community might have appeared from the outside, a rift began to develop between the Orthodox and *Neologue* observers. Similar political divisions existed between Croatian nationalists who considered themselves Jewish by religion, and Jews who were Zionist in orientation, although in both cases the former persisted in much smaller numbers.

Although Jewish organized community life developed along with a diversity of worldviews (e.g., political affiliation, field of activity, and religious ideology), Croatian law required all Jews to register with their local Jewish communities, regardless of ideology or field, in the nineteenth century. The law became problematic in several ways. First, it defined the Jewish community solely as a religious community, leaving little room for the rapidly changing interpretation of Jewish identity associated with nationhood. In addition, there were problems related to the ideological chasm between the *Neologue* and Orthodox observers and the relatively few individuals who defined themselves as Croatian nationalists of Jewish faith. Moreover, in Zagreb, as in other Croatian towns, the Jewish community was never visible in the sense that it had neighborhoods or streets, nor was it solely bound to "synagogue life." Even though the Jewish community was defined as a religious entity by Croatian law, services were meagerly attended in the *Praška* Street synagogue—a space that could accommodate only three hundred people in a community that at its height had eleven thousand Jews (I. Goldstein, 1998). The building itself is an example of acculturation patterns prevalent among Croatian Jews (R. Klein, 1998). The Moorish and Gothic features of the building reflect the relativist worldview of the majority of its community members. The Orthodox observers refused to participate in Jewish community activities along with non-Orthodox Jews. Accordingly, they held services in rented rooms, maintained their own cemetery, and operated a separate Talmud-Torah religious school. For the *Neologue* affiliated, the synagogue functioned as a social gathering place. As more facets of Jewish community life developed, members became involved in a wide range of Jewish organizations and, as a result, fewer Jews attended services.

Jewish organizations that emerged in the nineteenth century can be organized into four categories: humanitarian, intellectual, political, and recreational. Many of the organizations overlapped in their goals and interests. The common thread among them was that all provided a vehicle for members to be active in the Jewish community. The Humanitätsverein, or Humanist Society, was established in 1846. It was the first Jewish organization established after the tolerance tax was lifted (Kolar-Dimitrijević, 1998). The task of the Humanitätsverein was to organize and provide aid to the poor and elderly. The development of charitable organizations may be traced to the Judaic concept of *mitsvot*, which obliges Jews to an ethical duty of charity and *tikkun olam*, which reminds Jews of their moral responsibility of helping others and alleviating pain and suffering in the world.[4] The society was discontinued after just thirteen years of operation, but was reborn as the Jelena Priester Ladies Society in 1887, and was later renamed the Ženska Sekcija, or the Women's Division. In their continued effort to provide humanitarian aid, the Ženska Sekcija was very active during the 1930s, when Jewish refugees from Nazi-occupied areas fled to Zagreb. Other organizations provided humanitarian aid, such as the Local Committee for Aid to Jews from Germany, established in 1933, in conjunction with the American Jewish Joint Distribution Committee (JDC) and the Hebrew Immigrant Aid Society (HIAS).

At the turn of the century, a number of Jewish student organizations emerged. Among them was the Literary Meeting of Jewish Youth, which remained active until the outbreak of World War II, and the Zionist youth organization, *Hasomer Hacair* (or Young Guard), which held regular meetings in the 1920s. Both organizations were so successful in attracting youth that in 1906 the first Jewish newspaper, called *Židovska Smotra,* or Jewish Review, was established by the young members for those organizations. The community was becoming connected through the sharing of ideas. The weekly paper, *Židov*, or Jew, followed some ten years after the *Židovska Smotra* had been in circulation. *Židov* covered a wide range of topics relevant to the Jewish world, including what was perhaps the most important one at the time—Zionism.

The *Bar Giora* association of Jewish students emerged only a couple of years after the first Zionist Conference of South Slav University Students. Also established at this time were various Jewish national funds, which were indicative of the growing interest in Zionism. As Zionism became the most prevalent topic of discussion for European Jewry, *Hasomer Hacair* set out to prepare Jews for the departure to Palestine. Other Zionist organizations that prepared Jews for immigration to Palestine in the 1920s and 1930s included *Kadima* (or Forward), *Tehelet Lavan* (or Blue White—the colors of the Israeli flag), and *Erec* (or the Land of Israel). By 1940, roughly eight hundred members of these organizations had immigrated to Israel (Krauss, 1996). But while *Hasomer Hacair*, the most active organization, met on a regular basis, an anti-Zionist society called *Narodni Rad*, or People's Work, also met regularly. Led by a bookstore owner, the members of this organization did not want their children to be educated in the spirit of Jewish nationalism (I. Goldstein, 1996).

Some organizations were exclusively Jewish, such as the *Makabi* sport club, and the Israeli Youth Holiday Colony, which organized Jewish summer camps in Croatia.[5] Others, such as the Yugoslav Union of Cantors, were mixed. Among other organizations active in Croatia during this period were the Sephardi student society *Esperanza* and the previously mentioned independent Orthodox community, founded in 1926. International organizations reached the Jewish community as well. *B'nai B'rith*, or Sons of the Covenant, established a chapter in Zagreb in 1911. This organization attracted influential people whose objectives included the advancement of cultural, educational, and political life in the Jewish community. They organized distinguished tours and collected financial contributions for land purchase in Israel. The community had its own *hevra kadisha*, or holy society, that observed burial traditions. Membership in a Jewish organization began to serve not only as a way of belonging to a cultural and spiritual community (or to both), but also as a means for expressing political views and, perhaps most importantly, as a way of finding sustenance and community with fellow Jews.

## THE COMMUNITY DURING AND
## AFTER WORLD WAR II

With the outbreak of World War II, virtually all Jewish organizations that had been active throughout Croatia disappeared. It has often been said that European Jewry came together by meeting their fate during the Holocaust. This is true for the less than 5,000 Croatian Jews that survived the Holocaust. Of that number, about 2,500 were residents of Zagreb; others were either from smaller Croatian towns or refugees from abroad. Only 200 individuals returned from concentration camps such as Auschwitz, located in Poland, and Jasenovac, located in the eastern part of Croatia. Only 300 survived the war while living in Zagreb (S. Goldstein, 1998).

Many survivors are from intercultural marriages—a fact that has had significant repercussions for the continuation of the Jewish community. These individuals survived mainly because they were able to hide their Jewish background and "pass" as gentiles based on forged "Aryan certificates." In general, there are two types of survivors: those who hid or were able to pass as gentiles and those who fought with the *Partisans*, or National Liberation Committee. Those who fought with the *Partisans* and were lucky enough to survive developed a long-lasting loyalty to Yugoslavia and Tito. For the former, forced into passivity during the war, loyalty to the Yugoslav nation-state and Tito was not as important.

There are relatively few cases in which nonpersecuted Croatians protected Croatian Jews. Non-Jewish Croatians acting against the *Ustaša* regime risked persecution themselves. Jews who fled from the capital, where the hunt for Jews was the harshest, fled either to the Italian neutral zone (from 1941 through 1943) or sought refuge on Rab, an island off the Dalmatian coast. When Italy capitulated in 1943, many Jews fled to Switzerland for the remainder of the war (my grandfather was among them). But not everyone was able to successfully reach "neutral" Switzerland. Many refugees were turned away by the Swiss border control and met their deaths at the hands of the Nazis (Lengel Krizman, 1996).

Yugoslavia was dismembered at the beginning of the war in the spring of 1941. Much of the territory was divided among the Germans, Italians, and

Hungarians. The *Neovisna Država Hrvatska* (NDH), or Independent State of Croatia, was declared that year on April 10. The NDH was run by the *Ustašas* and controlled by the Axis powers.[6] Ante Pavelić, the commander in chief, modeled his totalitarian regime on those of Germany and Italy. In fact, the state parliament was not elected but appointed by Pavelić. By the end of April 1941, anti-Jewish legislation was in full operation. Two weeks after the NDH was proclaimed, all legal transactions with Jews were annulled. Jews were subsequently removed from public service and all other professions. Mandatory registration of Jewish property occurred in the summer of 1941, at which point over one thousand Zagrebian Jews had already been deported and killed. Prior to the arrival of organized concentration camps, the killings took place in mass execution centers. After most Jewish property had been seized, the remaining members of the decimated community were forced to wear yellow stars emblazoned with the letter Ž for *Židov*. The big round-up of Croatian Jews began as soon as the *Ustaša* liquidation system was set in place. Almost all Jews who had lived in Zagreb had been killed by 1942. The *Ustašas* worked in full compliance with the *Einsatzgruppen*, a special police force within Germany's *Shutzstaffel*, or SS police force, that helped implement the so-called Final Solution of the Croatian Jews.[7] Massive deportations to Jasenovac began in 1941. Jewish intellectuals are reported to have been among the first victims of *Ustaša* atrocities. Almost all members of the *Makabi* sports club and the *B'nai B'rith* society were arrested and killed. Despite the extent of murder, the *Einsatzgruppen* reported in 1943 that the *Ustašas* had not sufficiently carried out the Final Solution. As a result, the Jews that remained were deported to death camps outside of Croatia.

Croatians witnessed the events imposed by the *Ustaša* government. Although many watched in anguish, few were able to prevent anti-Jewish measures and deportations. Hiding or aiding Jews in any way was punishable by death. Stories of Holocaust survivors reveal the identities of those Croatians who fought against the injustice they saw committed before them.[8] Among them was Alojzije Štepinac, the archbishop of Zagreb, a person whose life story has caused controversy in the Jewish community. Štepinac was able to prevent the murder of fifty-five individuals living in a Jewish retirement home in Zagreb. Although Štepinac condemned the murder of innocent people publicly in 1943, he also supported the *Ustaša* government. In fact, many Serbs, Jews, and Croatian communists had already been killed before Štepinac spoke up. His anticommunist views, indirectly supportive of fascist doctrine, were articulated much earlier. In 1941, Štepinac was quoted as saying that the new Croatian state was the realization of a long-held ideal, without mentioning the fascist *Ustaša* rule that resulted from it.

The resistance movement was strong in Croatia. In fact, more Croatians joined the *Partisans* than supported the *Ustašas*. Their battle, in which about one thousand Jews were killed, lasted throughout the war. Early forms of resistance began as soon as the *Ustašas* had seized power. The aim of the resistance movement (at this time the National Aid [NA] campaign) was humanitarian in orientation and showed solidarity with all victims of *Ustaša* persecution. The NA operated in the winter of 1941, mostly in and around Zagreb; it included around two hundred grassroots organizations. Eventually, through a vast network of underground workers, the NA was able to merge into the *Partisans*. Finally, when the Germans were defeated in 1945 and the *Ustaša* government collapsed, the communist *Partisans* led by Tito came to power.

The Jewish community center in Zagreb had a somewhat different fate than public buildings in smaller Jewish communities dispersed throughout Croatia. *Ustaša* officials confiscated the community building in 1941 and used part of the building for the collection of Jewish property and other valuables. That same year, around one thousand kilos of gold were collected from Jews who were led to believe that by "donating" their assets they could save their lives (Strčić, 1998). In exchange, the *Ustaša* government, which later confiscated the gold and property, guaranteed those working in the office that they would not be deported and that the Jewish community could continue to function. In 1943, people working in the office started disappearing. Among them were Hugo Kon, president of the community, and Rabbi Miroslav Salom Freiberger. Kon perished in Jasenovac and Freiberger in Auschwitz. Although brutally reduced in numbers and impoverished, the community was able to remain active in providing healthcare to the needy and sending food packages to those detained in concentration camps. It managed to sustain itself with less than two hundred members, mostly individuals from intercultural backgrounds who were protected by the Catholic Church.

After the war, the much smaller Jewish community resumed. Subsequent waves of immigration to Israel and the United States in the late forties and early fifties further diminished the number of surviving Jews in Croatia to around 1,700, of which about 1,300 resided in Zagreb. Not all resumed community membership. Some who had been saved by serving the *Partisans* had developed a strong Yugoslav identity and did not feel the need to assert their Jewish heritage.

The diminished community, consisting primarily of members from intercultural marriages or parentage, met for social occasions at the ŽOZ community center and in smaller numbers to observe the High Holidays.[9] There were few organized outlets for Jewish education and religious practices. As Yugoslav society began to normalize, some Jewish cultural activities were restored. Zionist organizations were no longer in operation after the war, but the Moša Pijade, a Jewish choir that performed songs in Hebrew, Ladino, Yiddish, and

Serbo-Croatian, was reestablished.[10] Other cultural activities grew again, including an exchange with Jewish communities from Yugoslavia and neighboring countries, which involved excursions and summer camps for children and teenagers. In addition to the restoration of the kindergarten, much attention was given to the Jewish retirement home and other secular venues in the Jewish community. For example, a monthly community paper called the *Novi Omanut*, or New Art, began covering events pertinent to the Jewish cultural and literary world, the Ženska Sekcija resumed its activities and the youth continued meeting on a weekly basis.[11] Most Jews who remained in Zagreb after the last large colony of immigrants left for Israel and the United States were loyal to the Jewish community, to Zagreb, Croatia, and Yugoslavia.

## CONCLUSION

The history of Jewish community life in Croatia reveals its quintessentially urban, cosmopolitan, and integrated character. The expansion of the city of Zagreb, together with political changes experienced in the eighteenth and early nineteenth centuries, allowed for the development of an entrepreneurial class of Jews that included merchants and traders who would become industrials, bankers, and members of a learned professional class in the twentieth century. Economically inspired arrangements, such as the Edict of Tolerance, allowed for the development of a Jewish professional class. Although only a small number of Croatian Jews assimilated or maintained separatist lifestyles, most identified with and were active in Croatian economic, cultural, and even political life. The community as a whole was integrated but not assimilated, reflecting more general trends toward secularization. Acceptance in Croatian society was generally negotiated without compromising one's Jewish identity, due to Jewish social, political and cultural organizations. Nineteenth-century Croatian Jews were mostly employed in commerce and as professionals. They contributed beyond their numerical proportion to Zagreb's commercial and intellectual development and some became important city officials.

Examples of the continuation of the community can be found in the groups active within the *općina* today that organize a number of cultural events, much in the spirit of the Jewish literary organizations active before the Holocaust. These and other newer developments are discussed in subsequent chapters. The next chapter details the effects of the interwar period (1945–1991), the death of Tito in 1980, the subsequent disintegration of Yugoslavia, and the emergence of a xenophobic Croatia in the 1990s on the Jewish community.

## NOTES .

1. The *Neologue* (Greek for "new thought") movement, originating in Hungary in 1860, is associated with a branch of Judaism that emerged from the Jewish Enlightenment. Adherents to this movement were concerned with modernizing Judaism while at the same time preserving Jewish traditions.

2. A discrepancy exists between the number of members of Jewish communities dispersed throughout Croatia, national census data, and the actual number of Jews living in Croatia. This is due to fluctuating changes in cultural affiliation. I will discuss this in greater detail in the next chapter.

3. Ante Pavelić (1889–1959), who had been educated in Italy, played a great role in the import and materialization of fascism. He escaped to Argentina after the war where he lived out the remainder of his life.

4. The more general meaning of *tikkun olam*is is "repairing the world" or "making the world a right and better place." *Mitzvot* is the plural of *mitzvah*, which means "good deed" or "charity" or, less commonly used, "command" or "order." See Isaac Klein (1979) for a more detailed discussion of *mitswot ma'asiyot*.

5. The *Makabi* were a family of Jewish patriots of the second century B.C. They were active in the liberation of Judea from Syrian rule and appear in the story of Chanukah. The *Makabi* are remembered for their strength.

6. The Axis powers were a political alliance, which included Germany, Italy, Japan and other nations who opposed the Allies during World War II.

7. *Shutzstaffel*, or SS, literally means "protection squad" not "secret service," as commonly assumed.

8. The Jewish community honors those individuals who saved or attempted to save the Jews with Righteous Person certificates. The community continues to do so for all individuals or family members of those individuals until the present day.

9. The building of the Jewish community center in Zagreb was erected in 1898 at which time it was used as a primarily as a school and only secondarily as a community center.

10. Moša Pijade, Tito's right hand in Yugoslav politics after World War II, was the most famous communist revolutionary Jew.

11. Its interesting to note that *novi* means "new" in Croatian and *omanut* means "art" in Hebrew.

## Chapter Two

# The Rebirth of the Cultural Community: How Croatian Jews Derive Meaning from the Collapse of Communism

The collapse of communism in the late 1980s put into motion a transformation of cultural identities in Croatia and other former communist countries. A number of local and transnational factors made affiliations with ethnoreligious cultural communities in Croatia more appealing. Perhaps the most discernible alterations in cultural affiliation among Croatian Jewry have been connected with international efforts to boost collective Jewish consciousness and to local separatist movements, notably *Hrvatsko Proljeće*, or Croatian Spring, in the 1970s and Croatia's secession from Yugoslavia in 1991.[1] The separatist movement of the 1970s did not affect Croatian Jews in the same way as the post-communist era did, when the Jewish-Yugoslav symbiosis unraveled.[2] In the years following Croatia's transition from Yugoslavia, Jews began to be viewed as undesirable citizens and threatening to the new President Tuđman's national agenda. They were labeled as pro-Serbian, at a time when Serbs were considered Croatia's "natural" enemies, and as *Yugonostalgics*, or communist sympathizers, at a time when Croatia was trying to shed its communist identity and reinvent itself as a democratic, free-market state. At the height of Tuđman's xenophobic program, the imaginary "Jewish lobby" (perceived as operating locally and internationally) was blamed for having encouraged the international media and various human rights groups to keep a closer eye on Croatia's treatment of minorities. Exacerbated by *Ustaša* revisionism, Jews were denounced as either profiteers or pariahs of an unfair human rights watch that kept Croatia from joining the European community—a community to which many believed Croatia rightfully belonged.

31

In this chapter, I discuss the different ways in which the lives of Croatian Jews have been influenced by Tito's self-managing socialism (or *Yugoslavism*), Croatia's transition from Yugoslavia, and the more recent sociopolitical reforms in the 1990s. In the course of doing so, I posit that the tenuous Yugoslav position on Jewish matters led individual Jews to respond to Croatia's departure from Yugoslavia in a number of different ways. More specifically, because the Yugoslavian government condemned anti-Semitism (by making it punishable by law) as well as Zionism (by forming political alliances with the Arab world), worldviews about the desire to retain an outgrowth of *Yugoslavism* following Croatia's break with Yugoslavia were divided amongst Croatian Jews.[3]

One view, held predominantly by the older generation, can be described as maintaining the principles of *Bratstvo i Jedinstvo*—Tito's mythical Brotherhood and Unity that held the nation in a grip of idealized collectivity until Tito's death in 1980. Those in support of *Bratstvo i Jedinstvo* experienced Croatia's transition from Yugoslavia with a sense of loss and uncertainty. The other view, embraced by individuals across generations, endorsed the promise of democracy and the establishment of diplomatic relations with Israel as well as a hope for a better tomorrow. However, during the transition and its aftermath, when the experience of xenophobia and the construction of Jews as essential *outsiders* became a genuine concern, these seemingly fervent divisions evaporated.

## TITO'S YUGOSLAVIA

Yugoslavia was a federal state made up of six republics and built on the glory days of the *Partisans* who, under Tito's leadership, fought against the Axis powers (i.e., Germany, Italy, and the Croatian *Ustašas*) during World War II. The core of Tito's self-managing socialism, which emerged after Yugoslavia's break with Stalin in 1948, was the promise of a superior and more humane form of communism. After Yugoslavia's departure from the eastern block, Tito's main goal was the establishment of a distinctly Yugoslav national consciousness, which in time would dissolve primordial bonds (i.e., ethnic consciousness) and thereby promote the shared goals of the Yugoslav people.

Tito understood multiethnic Yugoslavia as a temporary state that would eventually dissolve. The ultimate goal, as he saw it, was for all cultural groups to fuse into a homogenous social unit. Tito was the symbolic patriarch and former leader of the *Partisans*, and the embodiment of *Bratstvo i Jedinstvo* that required intense levels of personal investment and political morale. His glorification played an important role in maintaining *Yugoslavism*. Although regional consciousness was never forbidden, it was only permitted so long as it did not challenge the regime or its ideal of national cohesion. As reflected in national census categories prior to 1961, alliance to Yugoslavia was not perceived as contradictory to asserting one's membership to one of the six republics. As a census category, the "Yugoslav" and "undecided" option was added only in 1961 (Sekulić, Hodson, and Massey, 1994).

Tito unwittingly encouraged ethnic identities to flourish by demanding unconditional loyalty to Yugoslavia while at the same time allowing the expression of regional identities. He mandated collective rituals intended to promote Yugoslavian unity, such as *Štafeta Mladosti* (or relay of youth), which involved the passing of a wooden baton from one cultural group to another. These rituals actually had the reverse and, in retrospect, unintended effect of underscoring the already sharp divisions between members of different ethnic groups. The vehement commitment to a political structure that kept the six republics functioning as an integrated whole and the ideological monopoly of *Bratstvo i Jedinstvo* was ultimately challenged. Along with Tito's death in 1980 and the emergence of *Glasnost* in the USSR came the reduction of state's security apparatus.[4] As a result, the affirmation of regional identities began to flourish, along with disparities in the distribution of wealth throughout the different republics.

Yugoslavia's ambiguity towards ethnic consciousness and minority cultures was reflected in its treatment of Yugoslav Jews. Although Yugoslavia condemned public anti-Semitism (making it punishable by law in 1945), and ranked among the first nations to recognize the state of Israel in 1948, the country's official policy was pro-Arab and anti-Zionist. During the Yom Kippur War in October 1973, six years after the country's diplomatic break with Israel in 1967, Yugoslavia officially aligned itself with the Arab world, and supported proclamations made by members of the United Nations that equated Zionism with racism.

Jewish support for Yugoslavia was complicated. Despite Yugoslavia's foreign policies, Croatian Jews continued to support *Yugoslavism* in addition to strongly identifying with the Zionist utopia (Freidenreich, 1984). This seemingly paradoxical set of beliefs can be explained by the fact that Croatian Jews had fought side-by-side with the *Partisans* during World War II and the fact that the new nation-states (Yugoslavia was established in 1945 and Israel in 1948) shared many historic, ideological, and economic similarities. For example, both Yugoslavia and Israel called for the unification of their people. Yugoslavia promised the integration of all classes through self-managing socialism, while Israel promised the integration of all Jews based on the principles of nationhood. Both states asked their citizens to help rebuild the

nation through voluntary service, both had been colonized for long periods
of time, both were constructed on strong ideals that helped establish their
independence, and both were dependent on the goodwill of their citizenry to
create their nations. Photographs depicting ordinary citizens helping to build
a road outside Zagreb illustrate the importance of collectivity and the perceived social rewards of communism. The Jews who helped to build that road
likely embraced both *Yugoslavism* and Zionism. Some immigrated to Israel
in the 1950s, working in collective campaigns to rebuild the nation. Others
remained in Yugoslavia and later participated in so-called working vacations,
where they joined kibbutzniks in "making the desert bloom"—a highly idealized collective movement established by Ben-Gurion, Israel's first prime
minister. The goals of social equality and liberation from discrimination were
powerful enough to motivate, and reactivate, cultural integration patterns
among Croatian Jews during the period of 1950–1985. Moreover, Yugoslavia's economy bounced back more rapidly than that of Israel, leading a number of Croatian Jews to return back home after having already made *aliyah*
in Israel.[5]

During Tito's Yugoslavia the Jewish community had officially been recognized as a religious community. This meant that compared to most other former communist countries in east-central Europe, Yugoslav Jews were allowed
to practice religion freely (Freidenreich, 1984). The law was reflected on the
national census administered in 1953, when over a thousand Croatian Jews
identified as Jews based on religion. However, when polled, only a few
claimed that they were observant—most had aligned themselves with communism (Švob, 1997). The fact that there were no full-time practicing rabbis
in the Croatian community between 1943 and 1998 was not due so much
to an imposition from the communist regime, but rather a reflection of the
acculturated character of the Jewish community, which had absorbed the
Yugoslav ideal of integrating or "normalizing" Jews into civil society.

The rise of Yugoslav self-identification among Yugoslav nationals on the
national census from 1961 to 1981 (from .4 percent to 8.2 percent) reflected
urban residency patterns, intercultural parentage, and alliance with *Yugoslavism* and the Communist Party (Petrović, 1983). Each of these factors can also
be used to describe Croatian Jewry during this period. However, the increase
in Yugoslav or regional self-identification in national census patterns sug-
gests more about the political climate in Yugoslavia at the time than Jewish
identity patterns. To illustrate, in 1971, during the first postwar Croatian separatist movement, 2,845 individuals in Croatia (the highest post–World War II
number) identified as ethnically Jewish (Švob, 1997). However, following the
events of the *Hrvatsko Proljeće*, the 1981 census revealed that only 316 individuals identified as ethnic Jews.

## TRANSITIONING FROM YUGOSLAVIA

Fear of the emerging political climate perhaps explains the 1981 national census. Although many Croatians regarded the *Ustašas* as a shameful reminder of their county's unresolved past the transition years have been described as a "dictatorship wrapped in the forms of democracy" the Tuđman era allowed for *Ustaša* revisionism to flourish. Under the pretext of "freedom of speech," the extreme right began to publicly speak of *Ustaša* ideology in neutral and sometimes even approving terms (Samary, 1995). The *Ustašas* were said to have embodied "a love for the Croatian nation." During Tuđman's Croatia, this was interpreted as healthy and natural. Dubravka Ugresić (1995) described Croatian responses to *Ustaša* revisionism and Croatia's transition from Yugoslavia as embodied in feelings of emptiness and stupor. For Croatian Jews the "never again" (an international slogan referring to the Holocaust and its aftermath) did not seem so certain anymore. After the fall of Yugoslavia and the subsequent emergence of *Ustaša* revisionism, such feelings of loss and disillusionment were widespread. Those who witnessed the transition recall a government responsible for removing the icons that had come to symbolize the ideology of the former regime, including monuments to the victims of fascism (Drakulić, 1997). For example, mythic Croatian knights and Catholic saints replaced the iconography of *Bratstvo i Jedinstvo*. Further, memorials honoring Croatian nationalists were erected, including a commemorative plaque honoring Stjepan Radic, an early supporter of Croatian secession whose political platform was built on anti-Semitism. In the early 1990s, memorials to infamous *Ustaša* were erected with Tuđman's approval, including those for Mile Budak (1945–1989), the minister of education during Pavelić's regime and an individual responsible for most of the deportations of the Jews, and Jure Francetić (1912–1943), who was responsible for the massacre of Bosnian Serbs and Jews.

For those Jews who held on to the principles of *Bratstvo i Jedinstvo* the meaning of nationhood and a sense of belonging had forever been altered. They described feeling an enormous void and sense of emptiness and confusion during the transition years. Those who endorsed the promise of democracy and a better tomorrow felt equally betrayed when they realized that the promise of democracy had failed to stem the rising tide of state authoritarianism, xenophobia, social inequality, and steadily increasing unemployment rates.[6] This was at a time when many people in their mid- to late-fifties were pushed into early retirement. The young were charged with reproducing the nation while the elderly were relegated to the margins of society and deemed "unproductive." The church had an influence in propagating the ideal of the new nation by outlawing abortion. The *općina* was filled with people who lost their jobs. They expressed feeling depressed about having too much time on their hands and too few assets to enjoy their retirement.

Despite the forced changes, ŽOZ members continued to uphold nostalgic images of Yugoslavia, claiming that life was good under Tito and that *"Bratstvo i Jedinstvo* is what we grew up with—it's all we have been familiar with all of our lives—it's what we are." Holocaust survivors who had joined the *Partisans* during World War II felt that they had lost all they believed in: "We gave our lives to the anti-fascist struggle. Now, all we believed in has been destroyed." Renaming the *Trg Žrtava Fašizma*, or Victims of Fascism Square, as *Trg Hrvatskih Velikana*, or Square of our Great Croatian Forebears, was another saddening experience, and not just for Holocaust survivors. Jadran, an intercultural Jew of Serbian descent who had witnessed the disappearance of a memorial to family members lost in World War II and had seen Budak's memorial erected in his birthplace (Sveti Rok), described feeling as if nobody cared about what had happened during the Holocaust: "It was as if people, by not protesting, somehow accepted what had happened." He said, "It was a scary time to be in Croatia. We did not know what would happen next. There were *Ustaša* signs and symbols everywhere, making the fear that the *Ustaša* regime would rise again very real."

For many, *Bratstvo i Jedinstvo* did not signify the good life. Those in support of the new democracy remembered being deprived of basic human freedoms, including the freedom to speak out against Yugoslavia's anti-Zionist politics. They also felt that Croatia's resources had been untapped or unfairly distributed among the former republics. Also voiced was the need for Croatia to join the European Union and commence the liberalization of free trade and capital investment. The communist system was described as old, outdated, and ultimately unsuccessful. These views were shared by the contingent of Croats from the Diaspora and their local supporters who understood Croatia's departure from Yugoslavia as an act of liberation from oppression. Croatian Jews who supported the emergence of the Croatian nation-state emphasized that the return of xenophobia and *Ustaša* revisionism was a result of Tuđman's government, not of what they understood to be the establishment of a free state. They believed that once the transition was behind them, Croatian society would stabilize and hate speech would be forgotten—there was a new day up ahead. Optimistic about the future of a market-driven and democratic Croatia, they pointed out that more Croatians fought against fascism during World War II than had joined the *Ustaša*.

The transition was a time in which the Croatian nation-state was imagined as an essential ethnic Croatian identity—a sentiment that would have a rippling effect on the Jewish community. One of the most prominent examples of this was the construction of linguistic differences between Serbs and

Croats, the two largest cultural groups in the former Yugoslavia. The perceived linguistic differences played a crucial role in formulating cultural distinction between Croats and Serbs. Croat nationalists emphasized differences between the "Serbian language" and the "Croatian language"—differences that linguists often describe as on the order of differences in dialects of a shared language.[7] Support for establishing Croatian as a separate language by eradicating Serbian words and reinstating "Croatian words" became one of the focal points of the nationalist movement. It gained considerable support from the Catholic clergy, which published a "Croatian prayer" using outdated language and sought to establish Catholic Croatian Day as a national holiday (Ramet, 1992).

The use of language for political means to create group cohesion and emphasize cultural distinction is not new. We have already seen that standard Serbo-Croatian, the official language of all former Yugoslavs, was established in the late nineteenth century during the conceptualization of the Ilyrian project. At that time, only slight linguistic variations existed between the eastern (Serbian) and western (Croatian) parts of the former Yugoslavia. The chief difference had to do with the use of different scripts (Cyrillic and the Roman alphabet), both of which were utilized during the formation of the Kingdom of Yugoslavia (1918–1941) as well as Tito's Yugoslavia (1945–1991).

Croatian independence campaigns (in the 1970s and most recently in 1991) also made use of linguistic differentiation programs, with the aim of *purifying* the Croatian language through the removal of Serbian, or non-Croatian, words.[8] During Croatia's secession from Yugoslavia, Croatian linguists were directed to educate the public about the use of Croatian and non-Croatian words in state run newspapers (Strčić, 1998). In its purified form, the Croatian language became highly symbolic of Croatian separatism and the reconstruction of political boundaries between the states. Similarly, the construction of a mono-ethnic space has been used to *purify* Tuđman's Croatia from its "natural" enemies (e.g., Serbs, which Tuđman proclaimed in a 1998 public address to be the genetic enemies of Croats). Scholars, writing about the myth of "ethnic purity," have argued that ethnonationalism would not be possible without the construction of ethnic distinction (Brass, 1991; Breuilly, 1994; Connor, 1994; Denitch, 1994; Eriksen, 1993).

After the initial stupor stage, Croatians began to voice their concern for the country's economic depression, its emerging essentialist agenda and its neofascist sympathies. In November 1996, as the voices of protest grew louder, masses of people, including many ŽOZ members, demonstrated against the HDZ government's attempt to shut down Radio 101, the country's only independent radio station. The demonstration was the largest public protest since

HDZ came to power in 1991. Under the threat of domestic and international pressure the government finally agreed to keep the station open. Inspired by this success, antifascists, former *Partisans*, and antinationalists gathered on Anti-Fascism Day in May 1998 around the *Trg Hrvatskih Velikana* to protest the name change.[9] There were several hundred people present at the protest, including some who cautioned that Croatia should not forget her anti-fascist identity.

Similar sentiments were echoed when Tuđman proposed erecting a memorial for the *Ustaša* that had fallen during the war, together with a memorial for those who perished in Jasenovac, a concentration camp established during the *Ustaša* regime (1941–1945). This was met with outrage from the Jewish community, which culminated in protest at the Mirogoj cemetery on Holocaust Memorial Day in April 1998. Representatives of a number of minority groups, including antifascists, former communists, *Partisan* fighters, Serbs, Roma (Gypsies), and Jews, delivered speeches calling for justice and respect for the memory of the victims. Protestors declared that the number of victims should not be underestimated (the death toll of the Holocaust had become a public debate throughout the former Yugoslavia, Croatia in particular) nor should the victims be memorialized together with their executioners.

In response to international concerns about *Ustaša* revisionism and Croatia's role during World War II, the petite Jewish Croatian community became newsworthy. The president of the community was often invited as a guest on televised talk shows and radio programs to discuss Croatia's role in putting World War II criminals on trial and securing the return of Jewish property through denationalization. The general perception in Croatia was that an international Jewish network of organizers and media people had soiled Croatia's reputation by dredging up the nation's troubled past. When I asked non-Jewish consultants how relations might be improved between the local Jewish community and the Croatian public, I was told on several occasions that the best thing individual Croatian Jews could do to reverse the international perception of Croatians as *Ustaša* sympathizers was to write about those Croatians who saved the Jews during World War II. I should note that the Croatians I spoke with were generally unaware of the Righteous Person award for Croats who had saved Jews during World War II. Although anti-Semitism, racism, or any other type of discrimination was officially censored and punishable by law in Yugoslavia, such laws were repealed as soon as the new regime came into office. Local politicians proclaimed Croatia's innocence and also claimed that they would protect "their" Jews. According to these politicians, the destruction of Jewish property during the Holocaust and in recent times (1991) was depicted as an act "against Croatian democracy," aimed to undermine the social order and slander Croatia's new image.[10]

News commentators depicted Croatia as the victim of Serb conspiracies. An official spokesperson for the HDZ proclaimed, "The destruction aimed at the Jewish community is in fact aimed at the Croatian people." The appropriation and destruction of Jewish property, seized and destroyed during the NDH and converted into state-owned property during Yugoslavia, was not described as an act of anti-Semitism or hate crime but as anti-Croatian and anticivilized. A religious leader proclaimed, "Those who hate Jews: hate mankind," and urged that Croatia needs to "show the world that Croatia is a place where freedom is enjoyed by all people." Those in favor of forgetting the past and striving toward the "new democracy" viewed helping the Jewish community to retrieve its property as positive for Croatia's political image. The return of Jewish property would convince the rest of the world that Croatians are not murderers engaged in genocide. According to the state-controlled press, the nation was "at this time in the process of stabilizing itself, moving towards democratic reform." Minority rights needed to be protected in order to secure Croatia's future entry in the European Union (EU). Social scandals such as the denial of basic freedoms, the government's attempt to shut down Radio 101, and neofascist allegations were deemed harmful to Croatia's ultimate goal of joining the EU. The overriding suggestion was that Jews were somehow to blame for all the negative media attention Croatia was getting. In the end there seemed to be a discrepancy between locally sanctioned anti-Semitism and the government's official policy illustrated in the notion of Croatia wanting to *protect their Jews.*

## TUĐMAN'S CROATIA AND THE
## EXPERIENCE OF ANTI-SEMITISM

Although Croatia incorporated nominal tenets of minority rights in its 1991 constitution, its critics have pointed out that these rights meant little more than a census category.[11] Striking evidence of this includes the obfuscation of the genocide committed by the *Ustaša* government during World War II and the "reconciliation program" proposed by Tuđman in which World War II victims and their murderers would be commemorated together. The resurrection of the political Right and the publication of several racist books, including the Protocols of the Elders of Zion, as well as and the government's official xenophobic policy toward "undesirable" minorities were reasons for great distress among Croatian Jews. Other incidents, such as labeling Croatian Jews as outsiders, *Yugonostalgics*, and Serb sympathizers and the denial of anti-Semitism in Croatia, were of serious concern to ŽOZ members. Many ŽOZ members also perceived Croatia's renewed diplomatic relations with

Israel as a way to dampen neo-Nazi accusations made against Cr·  aia by the international community. In their view, the˙ultimate aim of the media attention given to the *općina* was to whitewash the country's troubled history. Empathetic official support for the return of Jewish community property and public speeches that promised to *protect* Croatian Jews and cast Croats as victims, were additional sources of concern. Many Croatian Jews perceived the public speeches as paternalistic, and non-Jewish Croatians who associated themselves with the Jews in the name of justice and liberty were as opportunistic.[12]

ŽOZ members recalled a number of personal anti-Semitic experiences that labeled Jews as outsiders or, as someone put it, "undesirables." Ivana, an eighteen-year-old high school girl, was asked, "What do you Jews still want in Croatia?" Recalling an incident in 1991 at the Zagreb train station, a woman buying a ticket to Vienna was asked, "Are all you Jews escaping now?" But the same person also claimed that Jews are more frightened of anti-Semitism than what is really going on in Croatia which can perhaps best be described as xenophobia. The following remark, collected during an interview at the ŽOZ, illustrates this point: "Croatia suffers more from xenophobia than from anti-Semitism. The question now is, Who is considered an outsider?" One person felt that most xenophobic experiences are translated as anti-Serbian. When asked, many consultants explained that they have been labeled pro-Serbian. Maya's anti-Semitic experience at work in 1991 occurred at a time when many ethnic Serbs were fleeing Croatia. She was asked, "Don't you think that you should be leaving, too?" Miriam, a college student, explained,

> The way people treat the Jews is an indication of how they are conducting politics. I don't know how powerful the Jews really are in the world. As far as I know, people might be exaggerating. But the perception here is that being good with the Jews aligns Croatia with the West. It's possible of course; I am not excluding the possibility that Croatians really believe in justice for the Jews.

Another Croatian said,

> Croatia has never officially acknowledged the brutalities it committed during World War II. In the past we learned at school that the *Ustašas* and the *Četniks* were the same. But today, children only learn that the *Četniks* committed atrocities. So in the end, the *Ustaša* regime is portrayed as nothing more then a nationalist movement. In such an atmosphere, it is difficult to be tolerant of others.

Representatives of the ŽOZ have mostly been outspoken about anti-Semitism, but have not voiced their opinions on other issues related to Croatian xenophobia. On the contrary, the public image of the Jewish community is largely based on agreement with, rather than opposition to, the government. Compliance with local cultural norms has had a long history among Croatian Jews. The official response of community leaders is that while anti-Semitism exists in Croatia, as it does elsewhere, Croatians as a whole cannot be labeled as anti-Semitic. The Croatian government has responded to the Jewish community by sponsoring the reconstruction of the *općina* in Zagreb in 1991 and by reestablishing diplomatic relations with Israel. I asked interviewees if they thought a contradiction existed between Croatian (xenophobic) politics and government money allocated to ŽOZ. Most replied that they did not see it as a problem. In fact, some claimed, "Croatia owes it to the Jews."

## CONCLUSION

Three crucial influences have been discussed in regard to the changing meaning of Jewish cultural identification in Croatia. These are the collapse of Yugoslavia, Croatian separatism, and the reemergence of Croatian nationalism in the 1990s. During Tito's Yugoslavia, Yugoslavs remembered Jewish collective history because it was associated with the *Partisan*-led flight against fascism. In the postcommunist era, however, Jews were once again situated as *outsiders* and potential enemies of the Croatian national cause. Small in number, the presence of Jewish communities in Croatia appeared threatening to Croatian sovereignty only because such presence served as a reminder of the atrocities committed by the Croatian *Ustaša* regime. Responding to Croatia's negative exposure and international pressures, nationalist-oriented journalists set out to tell the "truth" about Croatia's role during World War II by portraying Croatia as the victim of the international media, the Jewish lobby, and the Serb conspiracies.

During its secession from Yugoslavia, Croatia identified Serbs and the memories of the former *Ustaša* regime as the enemies. At the same time, Croatia accepted nominal tenets of minority group rights that are incorporated in the Croatian constitution. Any association with Yugoslavia, communism, the international media, or the Serbs has been interpreted as directly antagonistic to Croatian sovereignty. The appropriation of Jewish community property was perceived as an injustice against Croatia, rather than an affront to the Jewish community. Perhaps well intentioned, the actions could not escape being seen as self-congratulatory propaganda about Croatia protecting her Jews and speeding up the return of Jewish property. Such a response reflects Croatia's Janus-faced political stance towards the Jewish community: diplomatic and nurturing before the lens of the international media while often indignant and suspicious at home.

The social and political organization of the present-day Jewish community is the subject of the next chapter. Tracing the memories of the *općina*'s past to the new meanings of the rebuilt community, we discover that much of the character and competing views of the Jewish community as described in this chapter has remained the same. Examining the community's varied manifestations and expressions provides useful insights into Croatia's changing political economy, (e.g., its transition from communism to capitalism, and the popular public debates that surround the changing meanings of community and Jewish identity).

## NOTES

1. The influence of international organizations in helping to foster a new vision of the postcommunist Jewish community was already evident during *Glasnost* and took root in Croatia in the mid- to late-1980s. These and other transnational factors contributing to the rapid transformation of Jewish communities in Croatia are discussed in subsequent chapters.

2. As we saw in the previous chapter, the first wave of Croatian nationalism dates back to the early nineteenth century. The first half of the twentieth century saw a succession of nationalist movements that led to the establishment of the Kingdom of Yugoslavia in 1918 and the Croatian separatist movement (1941–1945). The first separatist movement that called for the decentralization of resources and the amalgamation of Tito's Yugoslavia (1945–1991) dates back to the late 1960s. Although that project proved unsuccessful, in time it resulted in the secession of Croatia from Yugoslavia. Croatia's response to economic inequality during the interwar years (1945–1991), and its growing detachment from communist ideology emulated ideas held by many eastern block countries. More recent developments since the 1990s include an increasing idealization of market capitalism and an emerging self-perception of Croatia as a European Union nation.

3. Similar sociopolitical divisions emerged when a contingent of the Jewish Croatian community embraced the ideas of the Communist Party in the 1920 while another, the bourgeois entrepreneurs, began to subscribe to free-market ideals.

4. The *Glasnost* era is mostly remembered for the scrutiny it brought to the Stalinist system and communism in the former USSR. *Glasnost*, which means "clarity," was a policy introduced by Gorbachev in the mid 1980s that sought to liberalize the control of government information. Gorbachev and his aids reasoned that the liberalization of information would encourage support for the government's economic and social programs. Both *Perestroika*, which means "reconstruction" or "renewal" and *Glasnost* were policies that allowed for economic liberalization and freedom of expression.

5. *Aliyah* translates as "assent"; it is originally associated with individuals who are called upon to recite a blessing before the Torah reading. The contemporary meaning of *aliyah* is associated with the immigration of Jews to Israel. Jews who are said to have "made *aliyah*" (immigrated to Israel) are called *olim*.

6. For a discussion of the rising unemployment rates in Croatia, see Željko Rohantinski and Dragomir Vojnić eds., *Process of Privatization* (Zagreb: The Open Society Insti-

tute,1998). For a discussion of the rise in state authoritarianism and neofascism, see Živko Gruden, "What's in a Label and What's Behind It?" *Voice of the Jewish Communities in Croatia* (Spring 1996):13–15.

7. Nationalist Croats were not alone in this. Serbian linguists went to great lengths to demonstrate the exclusivity of the Serbian language. For example, the title of Pavele Ivić's *Srpski Narod I Njegov Jezik* (Beograd: Srpska Književna Zadruga, 1986) means "The Serbian People and Their Language."

8. The semantic similarity between *ethnicity*, *nationality*, and *nationalism* in standard Croatian usage reflects ambivalence toward these terms. Although cultural groups are occasionally viewed as belonging to distinct nations, nationalities, or national groups (Brubaker, 1996), these distinctions have no clear analogue in the Croatian language, where there are several ways of expressing the concepts of nation, nationality, ethnicity, and nationalism. The root for one set of expressions begins with *naci*, as in *nacionalnost* (nationality and/or ethnicity), *nacionalizam* (nationalism, nationalist feelings), and *nacionalna svijest* (national or ethnic consciousness). It might be revealing that the same root for expressing these concepts comes from the word *narod*, which refers to people, folk, nation, populace, or even mob, as in, for example, *narodni* (folk or national), *narodnosni* (ethnic), and *narodnjaštvo* (nationalism). Depending on the context in which it is used, *narod* may refer to either peoplehood or cultural minority. As Milica Bakić-Hayden (1992) puts it, *narod* raises problems similar to those encountered in the multiple meanings of the German notion of *volk*, which does not exactly translate to the neutral term of citizenship as it is often used, but to a specific ethnic, religious and linguistic group. The slogan *Smirt Fašizmu! Sloboda Narodu!* (Death to Fascism! Freedom to the People!), a popular closing for personal and business letters after 1945, exemplifies this nondistinction (here *narod* refers to people). Writing about the former Yugoslavia, Catherine Samary (1995) notes that, "in place of national minority the term 'nationality' was introduced (*narodnost* as opposed to *narod*—the distinction is difficult to translate)". The terms *narodnosti* and *nacionalnost* evoke dual affiliation with people and *volk*. Moreover, "nation" and "nationalism" are both synonymous with "ethnicity," a fact that makes the differences between these terms dubious and misleading.

9. Anti-Fascism Day was previously an official national holiday. The crowd demonstrated peacefully against the abomination of the victims of fascism and the war against fascism, while a smaller group singing *Ustaša* songs protested the gathering.

10. The Yugoslav government had made similar statements in the 1930s, assuring the Jewish community that their government would always protect them and insisting that Yugoslavia does not suffer from anti-Semitism (Freidenreich, 1984). Destruction of the Jewish community center in Zagreb and the Jewish cemetery is more fully discussed in subsequent chapters.

11. According to the Federal Bureau of Statistics, there were three options for those who declined to state their ethnic affiliation on the national census during the years between 1961 and 1981: (i) undecided, (ii) Yugoslav, and (iii) regional origin (e.g., Dalmatian, Herzegovinian, and so on). On the first postwar census (in 1953), only 413 individuals identified as "ethnic Jews," and 1,011 identified as Jews based on religion (Švob, 1997). Then, in 1961, the "Yugoslavs" and "undecided" categories grew and the Jewish-based-on-ethnicity category declined. In 1971, during the first postwar Croatian separatist movement, 2,845 individuals (the highest post-World War II number) identified as Jews in

the ethnic category in Croatia (Švob, 1997). Following the events of the *Hr...isko Prol-jeće*, the numbers for the 1981 census dropped radically when only 316 individuals identi-fied as ethnic Jews. In the national census in 1991, 600 identified as ethnic Jews and 633 as Jews in the newly available religious category, bringing the total number of Jewish ethnic and religious affiliation to 1,233.

12. A similar example is when Daniel Cohn-Bendit was denied permission to return to France in the late 1960s and protesters who empathized with Cohn proclaimed, "We are all German Jews!" (Finkielkraut, 1994). Associating with Jewish victimhood took on another more drastic form, namely, that of appropriating Jewish cultural symbols, for example, using the Holocaust to describe the murder of innocent people other than Jews or the use of the Star of David as a vehicle of communicating victimhood. In Kosovo in 1989, when Albanian miners struck against repressive policies, Slovenian politicians and intellectuals who sympathized with their cause used the Star of David to symbolize their resentment of the government's repressive policies against the Kosovars. Many older Yugoslavs associated the symbol with pain, suffering, and victimization (Gordiejew, 1999). The underlying message was that Jewish symbols and their connotation to victim-hood are no longer solely applicable to Jews—a message that emphasizes that non-Jewish Croatians are also victims.

# Chapter Three

# Institutions of Meaning

> The Belgrade [Jewish] community [center] is housed in an old building. The chairs and tables may not have been as nice as the ones in Zagreb, but when the first plane arrived from Sarajevo [during the war in Yugoslavia] with refugees we all made room for them in our homes. We treated them as our relatives. There was no question whether someone had enough room in their apartment, or if a person had the time. An apothecary and a kitchen were organized even before the war and basic supplies such as oil, water, sugar and flour were stored in the basement. Throughout the war about three thousand members received weekly packets with basic supplies.

The use of space described in this quotation reflects the role a community center can play in a time of crisis. It also exemplifies the identity of a community-based organization such as the ŽOZ in which members share a common sense of belonging and persecution, impending crisis and mutual responsibility. Interestingly, community members and their representatives gave a very similar description of the ŽOZ during the 1930s and 1940s.

The current view of the ŽOZ, as a site of social interaction and identity enactment, diverges substantially from the meaning of community in the quotation above. The postsocialist meaning of the ŽOZ is primarily experienced through identity politics and a constellation of divergent, often contested, meanings of Jewish identity. Yet the ŽOZ has also continued to function as a rallying place for the survival of Croatian Jewry, both in the immediate sense (during the most recent war in Yugoslavia) and through the efforts to reshape and preserve Jewish cultural identity.

In a postsocialist context, the ŽOZ can best be described as a "meaning-making institution" in which Jewish identity and the function of the community is being reshaped, contested, and negotiated. In order to illustrate how the ŽOZ has become a meaning-making institution, I examine the different uses of the ŽOZ space over time, pointing out how these uses reflect the various meanings imbedded in the sociopolitical climate that the ŽOZ inhabits.

In particular, I discuss the ways in which the social organization of the community is encoded in the organization of the physical space of the ŽOZ, and, moreover, how the changing meaning of Jewish community life is thereby renegotiated. The fact that the physical site of the *općina* shapes Jewish social organization and identity means that the possible relocation of the ŽOZ could have a significant and uncertain impact on the future of the community.

In discussing the social organization of the community, I extend the ideas discussed in the previous chapters by arguing that the social trends that characterized Jewish community life in the nineteenth century have persisted through numerous changes throughout the twentieth century. I posit that past and current stories about the ŽOZ indicate that Jewish community life continues to be defined in terms of social friendship networks and various types of cultural and political affiliations. Many of these narratives—including those about the new meaning of the rebuilt community space and the members' visions for a future Jewish community—reveal that the ŽOZ functions as the primary location in which Jewish community life is experienced, contested, and enacted. Examining these stories, I raise questions regarding the different expressions of Jewish identity in the community and the role of the ŽOZ in facilitating them. Extending the historical context of the ŽOZ to the sphere of social interaction, I point out that the community space in which Jewish identity continues to be revised is used ultimately for the purpose of expressing Jewish culture, providing a sense of renewal, and imagining the continuation of the Jewish community. Looking beyond the *općina* as a site in which social interaction and renewal occurs, I suggest that the social organization of the space provides useful insights into Croatia's changing political economy, from communism to capitalism, and the popular public debates that surround the changing meanings of community and Jewish identity. The rebuilt *općina* is also closely related to the memory of the Jewish community during the Holocaust.

## THE COMMUNITY THROUGH
## SPACE, TIME, AND MEMORY

The ŽOZ is located in the heart of Zagreb. Its massive gray stone structure stands six stories tall and almost half a city block long. Aside from a small security booth situated on the northwest corner of the building (added in 1992), the exterior of the building has changed very little since the turn of the nineteenth century. Completed in 1898, according to the designs of architects Honigsber and Deutsch, the building is reminiscent of the trend toward modernization prevalent in Croatia's urban centers throughout the 1800s. (Honigsber later became the president of the ŽOZ from 1907 to 1912.) Always in step with the popular trends of the time, the interior of the building underwent several reconstructions throughout the twentieth century. Early conversions occurred sometime in the 1920s and later in the 1960s. The most recent, and perhaps most dramatic, transformations were in 1991–1992.

These recent changes represent not only the social needs of the ŽOZ's members, management, and sponsors, but also the particular relationship the Jewish community sought to nourish with the society in which it is situated. An example of this is the ŽOZ's relationship with the city of Zagreb. In the 1920s, someone who pushed open the ŽOZ massive twenty-foot iron doors immediately saw a shield depicting the city of Zagreb in the foyer. In the 1950s, the same entrance revealed a photograph of Tito that replaced the shield, and in 1995, when I visited the community for the first time, the entrance hall displayed a large two-dimensional *menorah* donated by a local artist. Although the community had not distanced itself from the city of Zagreb or from *Yugonostalgia*, it had begun to embrace (and institutionalize) a different identity.

Past the *menorah* that currently graces the entrance hall are the offices of the president and vice president,·a large conference room, the administrative office, and the security guard's quarters. However, the administrative offices were not always on the first floor. A century or so ago, the administrative offices were very small and located somewhere on the third floor of the building. At some point the offices were moved to the basement, even further away from public access. This made sense since the prewar community did not host many events open to the public, and neither the mayor of Zagreb nor past heads of state ever visited the ŽOZ in those years. Before the current premier Mesić, the last head of state to visit the ŽOZ was Franjo Josip in 1895, a plaque commemorating his visit is posted in the foyer. Back then, the president of the community did not have a large separate office as he does today. The conference room and the administrative offices became important only in the years immediately prior to and after World War II, when a number of community members sought to immigrate to Israel and were in need of administrative assistance, and thus the offices became more accessibly located on the first floor.

The basement also underwent a number of structural changes throughout the years that came to signal the changing identity of the community. During my fieldwork, the basement was divided between a computer room, a small gym, and a ceramic workshop. The other half of the basement contained a kindergarten that has been in operation for over fifty years, an indication of the continued social and educational nature of the *općina*.

Between 1933 and 1941 a large part of the building was converted into offices that provided assistance to Jewish refugees from Austria, Germany, and former Czechoslovakia. Refugees received medical attention and care packages, as the Bosnian refugees did in the Belgrade community in the 1990s. The *općina* functioned in the 1930s as a transitional place, because Croatia was often the final destination of the refugees. While the *općina* remained in operation throughout the war, the school and all other cultural activities related to Jewish community life came to a halt. As soon as the war ended, the Jewish community focused its activities at the *općina* almost exclusively on caring for Jews displaced from Croatia and elsewhere.

Many Holocaust survivors had no place to go after the war. Those lucky enough to survive often returned to find their apartments occupied and their belongings stolen. Having fought in the resistance movement, Croatian Jews came home after the war in need of medical attention and financial assistance. Discovering that their families were either missing or dead, they turned to the Jewish community for aid. Consultants recall the *općina* as a boarding house for refugees after the war. The space where student activities were held (on the first floor, which continues to be the epicenter of administration the ŽOZ) was converted into a kitchen, laundry room, and a cafeteria. Refugees and other displaced persons with nowhere to go slept on the second floor during the months following the war.

The *Socijalna Sekcija*, or social welfare division of the *općina*, organized many of the activities described above. Significantly, in the 1980s and 1990s, the *Kulturalna Sekcija*, or the cultural division, acted as the principal designator of spatial use. During this time, the *Kulturalna Sekcija* was primarily concerned with strengthening Jewish cultural and religious identity and with helping to secure the continuation of the Jewish community. In light of these objectives, a separate space was created on the second floor. The current site for religious services, this space serves present-day objectives, such as the fight against the cultural assimilation of Croatian Jews. The *Miroslav Salom Freiberger* society, named after the last community rabbi, who perished in Auschwitz in 1943, is another example of a new cultural institution. Although the society does not actively rally to bring Croatian Jews "back" to the fold, it organizes cultural events, such as concerts, readings, films, and dramas based on Jewish themes. These events engage the audience in *Jewishness*. Other cultural activities, such as folkloric dance, ceramics, and courses in Hebrew and Jewish history (all of which emerged in the later part of the 1980s during the renaissance of the *općina*), serve a similar role in connecting members, visitors, and the general public with Jewish culture.

The increasing significance of the *Kulturalna Sekcija* should be viewed alongside wider developments in cultural awareness prior to Croatia's transition from Yugoslavia. Before the reconstruction of the interior in 1991–1992, both the community and the nation underwent a cultural awaking. In 1985, when Yugoslavia was still mourning the death of Tito five years earlier, Yugoslavs began to publicly question the social and ideological order of their nation. As their decreased leader's ideals of Brotherhood and Unity began to fade, a Jewish cultural educator was brought in from abroad to instill a different type of unity among Croatian Jews. The objectives were primarily to cultivate a sense of Jewish cultural pride and (appropriately, given the social political milieu of the time) a sense of "unity." Shula, the first and only cultural educator or *madriha* in the Zagrebian Jewish community, taught Hebrew, Jewish history, and religion. I met her in 2000 during her visit from Israel and asked her about the community in the early 1990s. Specifically, I wanted her to comment on how she perceived the use of the ŽOZ space. She said that the common gathering place for members and visitors at that time was the *klub*, a large elegant room on the second floor, which had become an emblem for educating people about their cultural heritage:

> The *klub* has always been an important gathering place for people in the community. But when I lived here something different was going on. The *klub* was the place where all the activities took place and the *općina* as a whole served to educate people about who they are. As a consequence, I think, I was rarely invited to someone's home during the four years I lived here. I think that was part of the process. I made many friends, but we mostly met at the *općina*. It was not only our socializing that brought us together, although that was an important part of it, but more importantly our common sense of belonging and our common goals.

Shula's personal goal was to educate people about Jewish culture, something she did with much gusto. She started a Saturday morning Torah discussion group and led candle lighting rituals on Friday evenings. She described the gatherings as very popular, attracting twenty or more people who would spend the weekend together to discuss Torah. She also translated articles from Hebrew to Croatian, including a booklet on kosher food, and organized a Sabbath observance in the community. I was told that over eighty people attended the first Sabbath. Shula also organized the first visit to the Auschwitz memorial museum in April 1989, as well as a number of "working vacations" for Croatian Jews to take in Israel during the summer.

Shula spoke about the community's renaissance as something that happened in the past and affected everyone in the community one way or another. However, during my research in the late 1990s, few signs of the renaissance described by Shula and others remained. Jewish educators had returned home, Hebrew classes attracted fewer and fewer students, and *Motek*, a Jewish youth publication to which many young people had contributed, had come to a halt.

How can the changes in the community's identity since the mid 1990s be understood? To answer this question, I examine the images of the community prior to and since the 1991 bombing of the ŽOZ, as described by ŽOZ members. First I set out to discuss the past images of the community. This is followed by an account of the social organization of the space as I witnessed it, and the first impression of ŽOZ members as they understood the meaning of the space.

## REMINISCENCE: IMAGES
## OF THE COMMUNITY

The ŽOZ was bombed on August 19, 1991, on the same night a memorial plaque for Holocaust victims located at the entrance of the Jewish cemetery in Zagreb was also targeted. The timing of these events roughly coincided with the fifty-year commemoration of the destruction of the synagogue in *Praška*, located two city blocks from the ŽOZ. The destruction of the synagogue in 1942 had been the most memorable destruction of Jewish communal property prior to the 1991 bombing of the *općina*. No other buildings in Zagreb had been targeted during the war in Yugoslavia. The origin of the explosion, which occurred at night when the ŽOZ was closed to the public, was traced to a trashcan left in front of the main entrance. The bomb destroyed the massive entrance door and did extensive damage to the ground and first floors.

There have been a wide variety of theories about the identity of the bombers and their objectives. One hypothesis is that the Croatian government was indirectly involved, and the bomb, set to explode in the middle of the night, was not intended to harm community members but to cause enough damage to the interior to require costly renovation. The government, which contributed generously to the renovation, was said to have used the occasion to display goodwill toward the Jewish community. Other explanations include Serb and Palestinian conspiracies. Regardless of the explanation, several things are certain: the ŽOZ undertook strict security measures after the bombing, the interior underwent major transformations, and members as well as visitors now view the *općina* as a different place.

After the bombing, an armed security guard was assigned to secure the premises twenty-four hours a day, and one has to pass through metal detectors and turn over one's bags for inspection before entering the foyer of the ŽOZ. In 1997, when I began my fieldwork, visitors were also asked to state the purpose of their visit. I clearly remember how uneasy the bulletproof glass, metal detector and security personnel made me feel. When I began visiting the *općina* on a daily basis, I was simply flagged through the security booth, often carrying paperwork, a tape recorder, and a large bag with my gym clothes. To this day, security remains tight. Visiting the ŽOZ still requires looking into a camera, and announcing one's arrival to a security guard prior to gaining entrance. The ŽOZ has security personnel on the inside and the outside of the building, and a twenty-four-hour surveillance system has been established. The guards who patrol the exterior of the building are paid with public funds. Additional armed security guards are hired to check bags and personal belongings during major public events, such as art shows, dance and music performances, or visits of high-ranking officials. All of these changes have resulted in visitors and members claiming that the ŽOZ "feels" different.

Aside from the enforced security guards the interior design and organization of the space has changed most dramatically in the *klub* on the second floor compared to the interior design changes in the rest of the building. After visiting several cultural community centers in Zagreb, I came to the conclusion that the ŽOZ has the most striking interior decoration. Although some consultants described the changes of the interior as favorable (i.e., they said that they enjoyed coming to the new center more than before), others felt that the spirit of the community was missing after the 1991 reconstruction. They claimed that after the reconstruction of the interior, the ŽOZ no longer felt Jewish. In their eyes, the space had become unfamiliar and elitist. Hanna, a Holocaust survivor, pointed to a large plush sofa and a massive cherry cabinet that stood behind the sofa: "See that area over there? That's where my bed was. That's where we lived after the war [in the latter part of the 1940s]. We were all refugees then. All we had back then were wooden benches and folding chairs, but it felt like home to me."

By asking consultants a series of questions regarding their experiences and memories of the *općina* before and after the bombing, I learned about the different ways in which the community is understood. Most people I spoke with thought of the *općina* as a place where they could find expression for their Jewish identity. The *općina* was rarely viewed as a social club divorced from a specifically Jewish community center. Yet Jewish identity embodied different meanings for different people. Social interaction with fellow community members, childhood friends, and a "Jewish atmosphere" were perceived as the most important reasons for visiting the *općina*. I heard different stories about first visits to the ŽOZ and a variety of views about the changes that had taken place in the community since the 1991 bombing. Consultants described the changing atmosphere in the *općina* as they had witnessed it over the years and spoke about the future of the ŽOZ.

Many consultants described the *općina* as congenial and "a good place to meet friends, read or have a cup coffee." Aside from the sociable atmosphere, the *općina* was associated with the "magic of the Sabbath" and, for older members, with memories dating back to college, high school, and childhood. As stated previously, some Holocaust survivors remember the cordial atmosphere in the *općina* right after World War II. Survivors emphasize the role of the Jewish community in getting them back on their feet during this time of crisis. Prior to the war, I am told, most Jewish families celebrated holidays at home after going to the synagogue in *Praška*. It was not until the 1950s that holidays such as Passover began to be celebrated in the *općina*, where members could have a Seder dinner together.

Lea, a Holocaust survivor in her late seventies who visits the *općina* every week for the senior gathering and the ceramics workshop, said that the *općina* was a better place for holiday celebrations than her home since it enabled her to be among friends and family simultaneously. She also pointed out that no one in her immediate family would be able to recite the appropriate prayers and that there was always at least one person in the community she could rely upon to recite the Hebrew prayers. Most individuals born in the 1940s remember being at the *općina* with their families after the war during the High Holidays when "freelance" rabbis from abroad visited and held services.

## FIRST IMPRESSIONS

I spoke with a great number of people about their first impressions of the *općina*, asking them to describe the first time they visited the ŽOZ. I have included the voices below as representative of different eras: the 1940s, 1960s, and the 1990s. The latter are adults who do not have a history with the ŽOZ and who discovered their Jewish roots sometime in the 1990s. I have also included the views of those who remain skeptics of recent returnees.

Vilko, a frail gentleman in his seventies, clearly remembered the *općina* in the late 1940s:

> I cannot recall my first memories because we would come here every day. I think I was in the seventh or eighth grade when we already started going to the *općina* by ourselves. We met downstairs in the basement every day where we played ping-pong, cards, and later soccer. Since you asked, a few days ago I looked through a bunch of pictures I have at home with a group of friends I know from here. I wish I had the photograph on me now so that I could show you how gray and dilapidated the walls looked. I remember water strains and it being cold in the basement. Not that we cared much about that back then. My earliest memories are of the Purim

performance we participated in. We ran up and down the stairs dressed up in costumes. That's what I remember.

Vilko stressed the fact that the community, that is, his friends in the community, have been part of his everyday life for almost three quarters of a century. His memories of the *općina* are reflected in the friendships and the social relations he established in primary school and continues to nurture as an adult. He emphasized that his friends give him a sense of history in the community.

I met Danijela at the seniors' gathering. Like Vilko, her closest friends are those she met in the community. Danijela's story is one of a kind because she literally grew up in the *općina*. She shared some of the childhood memories described by Vilko:

> I was born in Split [a medium size town on the Dalmatian coast] in 1939. When Italy fell we had to flee from Dalmatia, since we lived in Split and lived in the apartment adjacent to the Jewish community because my father was a cantor. We left Split when my dad got beaten and they completely demolished our apartment in 1942. After we left the synagogue, everything in it was burned. We fled and joined the Partisan refugees' camp and from there we left for Italy. From Italy we went to Africa, instead of America, and came to Zagreb after the war ended. My father decided to move us to Zagreb after the war because he was looking for work. He found employment in the ŽOZ, where he moved us in 1950. I remember it exactly because it was New Year's when we moved into the ŽOZ. We lived where the [administrative] offices are now, on the left side, when you enter [the building]. The synagogue was on the right side, and on the left side was our apartment. My father came from a family that was religious so he knew all of those prayers. He sang very nicely and soon after we arrived he was put in charge of the service on Fridays and on all of the holidays. Sometimes a real rabbi from Hungary or from somewhere would come here, but dad did all the other duties starting from birth to death. Unfortunately, there were many funeral processions where he was needed. He worked until he got sick in 1970. He died in 1972.

The synagogue space Danijela described was eventually moved to the second floor to make space for the current location of the offices of the vice president and the president and the conference room. Above all, Danijela explained that the organization of the space was much less formal at that time than it is today.

Descriptions of the *općina* as a place in which friendships are made and holidays are celebrated are also echoed in the stories of the 1960s. Ljerka, who loves telling people about her son who lives in Israel and has married a Jewish girl, remembered the warm atmosphere at the *općina* in the 1960s. "Since most of us did not own a television, we met at the *općina* on Wednesday nights to watch television together. But we also met on other nights just to hang out and eat sandwiches." Ljerka smiled, "I remember they had the best sausages in town!" She explained that pork sausages are no longer allowed in the *općina* since the koshering of the ŽOZ (more about this in the next chapter). Ognjen, a busy surgeon and the president of the ŽOZ who I have only seen wearing a suit, has, similarly to Ljerka, nostalgic memories about the sausages. Ognjen described his experiences at the *općina* as mostly social: "We played ping-pong and listened to the Beatles on Wednesdays back then." Sanda, who was almost always present at the *općina* during my fieldwork and whose parents were active in the community in the 1960s, said that she could hardly wait for the summer so she could spend most of her time with people she got to know in the *općina*. Sanda said that the majority of her friends are ŽOZ members. Engaged in a number of social activities ranging from the responsibilities associated with the Ženska Sekcija, to service on the board for directors, Sanda continues as her parents before her to maintain an active role in the *općina*. I asked her to tell me about the first time she visited the *općina*:

> I cannot really answer that because I grew up in our *općina*. I attended the Jewish preschool, so that is an important part of my growing up and my life. There is no beginning or first time. The *općina* is and continues to be always present for me. I started attending preschool in the community. I think I was three or four years old, that was in 1953 or 1955. The preschool was not in this building like it is today but in *Tomislavov trg* 4. We learned songs in Hebrew that I still remember. The *općina* was my world—it still is. I did not learn about Judaism from my mom's stories or from my grandmother but I grew up in it. I actually think that that is the best way to learn. I am very much against introducing mandatory religious studies in Croatian preschools unless they are multicultural because I know what it is like to learn about your own culture in preschool. It's an incredibly important time period for a child's development. I do not remember other things from my childhood from that point in time, but I remember the preschool and the events, the songs we learned, the movies we watched. I remember the cartoons and the toys that we had. Did you know that Joint (*American Jewish Joint Distribution Committee*) bought those toys? They were American toys—it was the only preschool in Zagreb that had something like that. I mean, there were no real cars in the streets here, let alone toys. This is why the preschool we have here is very important for the continuation of our community. Children need to attend the preschool of the milieu to which they belong so that they don't get indoctrinated with something else.

Sanda stressed education as the most important component to maintaining Jewish community life. The community space, she said, is best used for educational purposes that promote cultural awareness and understanding. She feels that she has a common sense of belonging with fellow community members because she shares educational experiences with them.

Ana was very self-conscious about her Jewish background. She was described by my English students as being vague about who, if anyone, in her family was Jewish. I spoke with Ana after class one day when she told me about her first visit to the *općina* in 1992. Her experiences of her young days were very different from those of Vilko, Danijela, Ljerka, Ognjen, and Sanda. She said that she did not know Jews gathered at the *općina* until she was in her mid-forties. She emphasized that the revival years brought many people to the *općina*. Some members, she recalled, broke their parents' patterns of identifying as communists and Yugoslavs rather than Jews. Ana recalled her first visit to the Jewish community center:

> I did not grow up Jewish. I was shopping downtown with my son a couple of years ago during the war [in 1992] when the air raid sirens went off. Most people ran for shelter to an underground tunnel on the main square. We were only a couple of blocks from the *općina*. I had wanted to visit the *općina* but had never been there before. I think I had only recently found out about the *općina* at that time. Among all the chaos and confusion around us it seemed like the right time to go. So, we rang the bell as the sirens were still going strong and joined a couple of people who were in the middle of a religious service.

The religious service Ana described was held on the third floor. Ana described the place as bright, warm, and inviting. She remembered feeling at home instantly.

Like Ana, Ljerka first came to the *općina* as an adult. She told me about her "return" to the Jewish community and her first impressions:

> Tuđman's war left me feeling like I was in a vacuum. I felt lost. I could not believe my eyes and ears. When the craziness began, I fled to where I knew I would be safe. *Ustaša* songs were sung on *Ban Jelačić* at the time by men dressed in black and wearing baseball caps bearing the letter *U* [for *Ustaša*]. I could not believe all this was happening. Tuđman brought me back, in a sense, to where I belong. My first impressions of the *općina* were those of safety. The building looks to me like a strong large rock. I can barely push the door open by myself. Inside I feel safe.

The main difference between the stories told by Vilko, Danijela, and Sanda and those of Ana and Ljerka is that the latter had no personal history with the community or with Jewishness in general before they encountered the ŽOZ. There are many reasons for their desire to belong and become engaged in the Jewish community in addition to the void many Yugoslavs felt during transition and the trying time of the Tuđman regime. The oft-repeated sentiment of those who came to the *općina* as adults is that membership gave them a sense a security and belonging.

Although it is the minority view in the community, not everybody was accepting of people who discovered their Jewish roots later in life. Some viewed these individuals as profiteers. Davor, someone who ironically discovered Judaism later in his life and would describe himself as an observant Jew, expressed skepticism about people like Ana and Ljerka, whom he called *novo-komponirani Židovi* (newly composed Jews). Davor was equally disturbed about what he called the "ecumenical atmosphere that came to dominate the *općina* after its reconstruction in 1992." In his view, the community's interior was looking elitist and thereby not representative of an "authentic Jewish spirit." In his opinion, in order to retain its original "spirit," the ŽOZ needed to remain autonomous and set apart from Croatian society. Having to rely on governmental and international support had altered the "spirit" of the community. He insisted that the ŽOZ's lenient policies towards its members and the wider public encouraged Jews to pick and choose their Jewish identity—something he viewed as the beginning of the demise of the community. Here is how he described the changes in Jewish community:

> Catholics are studying the Torah at the ŽOZ and being Jewish has somehow become fashionable. There is something decadent about Jewish identity today. I am personally interested in studying the Torah as a foundation for a way of life, a Jewish way of life. This is different from the way the new Jews are studying Torah. Torah cannot be taken in small doses or modified. How can someone be a good Jew if he does not obey Jewish laws? Some people here have a lot of knowledge and are dedicated to Judaism. But the fact remains that *goys* [non-Jews] are shaping the Jewish spirit at the *općina*. The architects who redesigned the interior are not Jewish. If you ask me, they omitted the Jewish soul from this place. There is an elite feel to the decoration of the interior, which is contradictory to a Jewish way of thinking. Our community has become outward-centered, instead of being concerned with itself, as it had done for centuries. [Slavko] Goldstein's "open house" policies were outward-centered and decadent. The general perception is that Croatian Jews are prosperous, which is very different from the actual situation. A middle class in the economic sense no longer exists in Croatia and Jews are not part of the group who got rich during the war. Not everyone is rich; many cannot even afford to pay membership fees. But because of the outward-centered image, the Jews here are untruthfully represented.

Associated with the outward-centeredness that Davor described is the renaissance of the community, which, as he saw it, is directly connected to the money the community received from the Croatian government. In the view of those who share Davors's perspective, government money that was given to rebuild the community after the bombing changed the image of the community by giving it an elite appearance. While it is true that since the reconstruction of the ŽOZ's interior the *općina* has been known for its elegant design and congenial atmosphere, this is hardly the only reason why *novo-komponirani Židovi* and others have been attracted to the Jewish community. Many others saw the *općina* as less attractive since it was been rebuilt and felt that part of the old community was gone forever.

## THE SOCIAL ORGANIZATION OF THE REBUILT COMMUNITY: THE ŽOZ'S RANGE OF ACTIVITIES

Although the ŽOZ shares some qualities with other community organizations, the *općina* is truly unique. What makes the *općina* distinct is the ways in which many different and competing aspects of Jewish community life may be experienced under one roof. It is a center of learning, play, and appreciation of the arts as much as a sanctuary from everyday life as well as in times of social upheaval and political crisis. This diversity is depicted on the announcement board located in the foyer that lists an array of upcoming events at the ŽOZ, including high holiday observance, the monthly Family Sabbath (which I was told originated in Zagreb), and a variety of other social gatherings organized by the *Miroslav Salom Freiberger* society. Information regarding conferences on Jewish topics, excursions to Jewish communities abroad, and obituaries is visible on the wall by the massive staircase leading to the first floor.

The second floor, where the *klub* and the adjacent 150-seat theater are housed, is considered the hub of activities. The *klub* is a large, beautifully lit room with a piano, a television, several comfortable couches, small coffee tables, and chairs. It is used for a variety of social events. Large Chagall-like paintings and tapestries depicting Jewish themes, donated by a local artist, cover the walls of the *klub*, giving the place a congenial atmosphere. During the day the *klub* functions as a café where members of all ages meet friends for a drink or *strudel*, made right in the new Kosher kitchen of the *općina*. The space is also used for the monthly Family Sabbath and other social gatherings, such as the Ženska Sekcija, the Jeri klub for seniors, and the omladinski klub, or youth group. Films, concerts, and various other activities requiring a seated audience are held in the theater adjacent to the *klub*. The synagogue, the library, and the *učionica*, or education room, where most language classes are held, are on the third floor. Additional offices, a ping-pong room, and a space for dance practice (which doubles as an art gallery) are on the fourth floor. In the late 1990s, the *općina* offered courses in basic computing skills, folkloric dance, music, ceramics, foreign languages such as English, and activities related to Jewish themes, thus providing consultants different ways in which Jewishness could be experienced. The ceramics workshop, for example, encouraged consultants to make *menorahs* and other

*Judaica* objects, instead of those unrelated to Jewish culture or Judaism. Ultimately, the choices were discretionary, but most potters seemed to follow a
pattern that incorporated Jewish cultural themes. In contrast, observant individuals sought to express Jewishness in what they believed to be a more traditional assertion, and they abhorred the recreational workshops. In their
opinion, people should be learning about their Jewish heritage through other
means, principally through studying Torah.

The variety of views described above echo the long tradition of Jewish
Croatian organizations divided by humanitarian, political, intellectual, and
recreational activities. Like today, competing ideas about national politics
and Jewish religious practices coexisted in the nineteenth century, when a
number of organizations emerged to accommodate the different expressions
of Jewish community life. Although the Jewish community is much smaller
today, separate coalitions continue to reside within the *općina* to accommodate the different expressions of Jewish identity that are being negotiated at
the *općina*. However, it is important to note that ultimately there were no real
schisms between the members. In fact, for all the symbolic boundaries that
seemed to exist between them, a sense of unity dominated.

Today, the ŽOZ is home to a range of subgroups, each of which has different ideas about the uses of the ŽOZ space, Jewish identity, and the meaning
of the community. The most prominent social groups at the ŽOZ are the folklore troupe, the Jeri klub, Ženska Sekcija, and the religiously observant.
Other groups that meet regularly in the *općina* include the omladinski klub,
students from the Hebrew and English language classes, and the ceramicists.
Some of the social activities of the groups overlap. For example, a large number of individuals in the Ženska Sekcija also attend the weekly seniors' meeting. Similarly, many students of Jewish folklore and Hebrew also attend the
youth group meetings on Thursday nights, and those who study English often
attend the monthly Ženska Sekcija. However, a great number of members are
*klub* goers who rarely attend any of the group meetings except for the occasional *Miroslav Salom Freiberger* presentation or the monthly Family Shabbat. The religiously observant members normally attend Shabbat services and
other Jewish holidays only on Friday evening and Saturday morning.

*Dance*

Despite the fact that I was once told in New York by a Turkish belly dance
instructor that I have "no rhythm," I decided as a good participant observer
to join the folkloric dance class offered in the *općina* every Thursday night.
I was able to join the group in 1997, when it was newly established and when

many amateurs and un-rhythmic persons such as myself were not shunned. At that time, young women, some young men, and a few older (fifty and over) women attended the dance classes. I remember distinctly that the music (Israeli and Middle Eastern) and young dancers attracted an audience on Thursday night when the youth groups and others met. Depending on the preparation of upcoming events, the folkloric dance troupe currently meets several times a week. Over time, the dancers became younger and more professional during the years and the repertoire more serious. But the music and the laughter did not disappear.

In my conversations with the young dancers, I discovered that many strongly identify as Jews (not all dancers are Jews or members of the ŽOZ), yet they show no particular commitment to practicing Judaism and seem to regard the congregation as narrow-minded and conservative. The dancers were mostly interested in learning more about Jewish folklore and culture through dance. Some visited Israel and participated in various seminars related to the Jewish world, while others took Hebrew language classes. The dance instructor echoed similar ideas. She understood the folklore class and the use of ŽOZ space for these purposes as a means for young people to get involved with their Jewish heritage: According to Neda, an unusually energetic and motivated woman in her fifties, individual expression of Jewishness is associated with something she calls, "learning to be Jewish"—that is, learning the meaning of Jewishness through dance. Neda was able to combine her passion for Jewishness and folkloric dance, the two very meaningful aspects of her life she rediscovered in the 1990s. She lived her Jewishness and engagement in the *općina* largely through dance. Neda explained to me that in the context of the Jewish community, the dance troupe is concerned with the ways in which dance represents the Jewish community to the outside world. This was perhaps most noticeable at the first Croatian Minorities Celebration festival in 1998. Modern Israeli dances were performed at this festival. The reason for this, Neda explained, was because there are no specifically Croatian Jewish dances. The decision to use modern Israeli dances was decried by a number of members. One consultant claimed that Israeli dance was not representative of the Jewish Croatian community. Someone else claimed that "our community has no history in folk dance and Israel is too young a state to have folklore." These individuals said they would have preferred traditional Eastern European Hasidic dances or no dances at all.

The absence of such a historical precedent (a Jewish dance troupe did not exist in Croatia from 1938 to 1995, and prior to 1938 the troupe was not considered "professional") can be viewed as an opportunity to experiment. "Jewish identity is after all being reinvented here," someone from the dance troupe said. Choosing to perform modern Israeli dances at the Minorities Celebration festival reflects the diplomatic policy adopted by Croatia towards Israel. Alternatively, the ŽOZ's choice of dance repertoire may be an indication of the desire to reconstruct the meaning of Jewish identity in Croatia.

## Language

Language courses, including several levels of Hebrew, were held weekly in the small study adjacent to the synagogue on the third floor. A large conference table with comfortable chairs dominated the space. Hebrew lessons were popularized in the mid-1980s as Jewish educators were brought from Israel, and for a few years in the early- to mid-1990s, courses were overflowing and several additional levels had to be introduced. But in 1997–1998 that trend was reversed, and Hebrew courses were only mildly popular. Most of the Hebrew students I met said that they had studied the language for several years but had learned very little. They claimed that their participation in the course was largely recreational. In comparison to Hebrew, the weekly English language course has been consistently popular since the 1990s. Those who grew up during Tito's Yugoslavia had the choice between Russian and French as their foreign language requirement in high school, but when English became the language of diplomacy, those choices seemed outdated. Sometime in the 1980s, when Croatian high school students began studying English in school, the foreign language gap between them and the older generation began to widen. The ŽOZ was viewed as a place that could accommodate, and partially subsidize, the interest in learning English.

To accommodate the demand, I was asked to teach an English conversation course. My course attracted thirteen older women between the ages of fifty and seventy who had time on their hands, were involved in other activities in the ŽOZ, and who did not have much opportunity to study foreign languages during their working years. We met once a week to discuss topics relevant to the Jewish world, but the students stressed that their participation in the course was primarily recreational and that the occasion offered them a chance to catch up with old friends. For me, it was an opportunity to get to know community members more intimately.

Sitting down to coffee in the *klub* was an obligatory ritual after class. All my students were curious about Jewish culture and tradition but none were religiously observant. Jewish recipes from around the world were an especially popular topic of discussion. "Jewish food" was debated and understood in different ways (e.g., whether it is defined by Israeli cuisine, which was viewed as "too spicy and too foreign for our Balkan tastes," or defined by kosher dietary laws). The dominant view of the students was that kosher food and laws are impractical and, as one student put it, "irrational." The same student pointed out that "Jewish food" is an amalgamation of different recipes from places around the world where Jews used to live. Similar lively debates followed when we discussed articles that described the changing meaning of Jewish social life.

## Ceramics, Seniors, and Conversation

Like the language class, the ceramists met once a week. Located next to the computer center in the basement, the ceramics workshop was comprised of one room housing a kiln donated by a local potter, and another workspace with a large table and several shelves for displaying finished works. The ceramics students largely envisioned the *općina* as a place to make and sustain friendships and to become involved with Jewish culture on some level, but the ceramics workshop also attracted a number of women outside the Jewish community. Coffee and cakes brought by group members were always served during the workshop. One day the rabbi visited the workshop and suggested that the artists make several thousand *mezuzot* (small ceramic or wooden fixtures which hold miniature Torah verses and are attached to doors of Jewish houses) and sell these to ŽOZ members for profit. The idea was perceived as absurd by the artists, since the group met primarily for socializing.

The senior group also met once a week in the *klub* on the second floor. The senior gathering was semiformal and organized around discussions of subjects related to the Jewish world. The *općina* was the locus of many seniors' world: it was where they met their childhood friends and the place they kept their memories alive. Each week a speaker from within the group prepared an informal presentation, usually a reading or translation of a text followed by a discussion. Topics like the war in Yugoslavia and the brutalities of the Holocaust were typically avoided. Instead, discussions focused on a bygone era and the wider Jewish world. Jelena, the coordinator of the senior group, said that she did not see any point in turning the meeting into a "griping session" about memories of the Holocaust or the trials and tribulations of old age. She maintained that the function of the group was to challenge a person's intellect and share in each other's company. "There are different outlets for those wanting to talk about their experiences during the Holocaust," she said, pointing out that most elderly members had participated in a Steven Spielberg Foundation video interview documenting the histories of Holocaust survivors. Discussion themes in the senior group ranged from recollections of personal events prior to the outbreak of the World War II to Jewish newspaper articles from that period and events in the wider Jewish world. Most seniors described themselves as secular Jews who were predominately interested in keeping their "minds active."

## The Observers

The religiously observant were by far the minority in the ŽOZ. Worship services were held every Friday evening, and Torah reading and discussion occurred on Saturday mornings. All of these meetings took place on the third floor of the *općina*. A special room was designated for worship. The west wall of the room was draped with modern silk fabric donated by an Israeli family. A lectern faced southeast toward Israel, and Torah scrolls behind the lectern marked the south wall. An Orthodox rabbi who visited the community several years ago suggested an Orthodox-style gendered division of both the synagogue space and the adjacent study. Men were assigned to the east side of the room and women to the west.

Apart from the Sabbath, observed every Friday night, the adjacent study was also used for holidays, typically drawing a much larger crowd. Large swinging French doors separated the synagogue from the study. On the more crowded holidays, such as Rosh Hashanah (Jewish New Year), Yom Kippur (Day of Atonement), and occasional wedding ceremonies, the doors were kept open, extending the space to almost double its size. At this time, additional rows of chairs were added to the hallway in between the study and the synagogue.

Services in the ŽOZ were always performed in Hebrew, a language very few worshippers understood. Some congregants sang along with the prayers, admitting that they did not understand the words. Nevertheless, partaking in the service offered many ways of expressing Jewish identity and being involved with the Jewish community. For some, this meant simply absorbing the sound of the prayers, reading along with the spoken text (a Roman alphabet reader was available) and sharing in the experience with others. Most congregants moved into the adjoining study after the Sabbath service where *Kiddush* (blessing over wine) was said and the *Parasha* (the weekly portion in the biblical Torah) was read. Community matters and upcoming events were also addressed at this time. Occasionally, media events concerning some aspect of Jewish culture were debated.

Prior to the arrival of the rabbi in 1998, a self-appointed leader named Nicola held Torah study and worship services. Nicola is a retired electrician in his sixties who acted as the *Hazzan* (someone who recites the liturgical prayers) as well as the discussant. Nicola always had a kind word for everyone it seemed. He conducted services in his "uniform"—Levi jeans pants and jacket and a baseball cap—and was generally an easy going and kind person. He was self-taught in Hebrew and English and spent time at a *Yeshiva* (a Jewish religious school) in Israel. He had "come to Judaism," as he put it, sometime in the mid 1980s, inspired by Shula, the Israeli *madriha*. His growing interest in Judaism occurred slowly and mostly after Shula left. Nicola articulated the ŽOZ's primary goal and function to me in one of the many conversations we had during the Saturday morning Torah studies I participated in during my time in Zagreb. According to Nicola and the religiously observant members, the "Jewish community" was understood as a community of worship. Although Nicola was largely perceived as "easy going," he did not accept a different interpretation of the ŽOZ. In fact, an alternate interpretation of the "Jewish community" was for the most part understood as inauthentic by the religiously observant members of the ŽOZ. Although these members gathered out of a genuine interest in Judaism on Saturday morning for the Torah reading and discussion, they recognized that their gathering was also for sociable purposes. Discussions on Saturday morning were energetic. Most discussions revolved around Jewish religious law, and topics ranged from Orthodox responses to evolving gender roles to social and political problems in Israeli and Croatian society. The atmosphere was generally lively and good-spirited, though a newcomer might perceive the congregants as argumentative.

One topic that regularly sparked argument was proper behavior during worship service and Torah study. Some believed it ill-mannered to converse with fellow observers during such services. Yet others were convinced that such acts are quintessentially Jewish. Mirna, a petite woman in her forties who had spent several years studying in Israel, said that socializing with fellow congregants during the service was an "authentic Jewish" practice. She noted that talking during the Jewish service sets the service apart from the comparatively austere Catholic service. She believes observers are supposed to be joyful on Sabbath, not somber. Further benign conflicts arose about the *true* meaning or authentic practice of Judaism. Congregants often emphasized their already predictable views in those debates focusing on the *authentic* meaning of the *Parasha* and interpretations of Jewish religious laws and their historic meanings. The amicable nature of such heated discussions is well illustrated with a joke Nicola told:

> When the *Shema* prayer was said, half of the congregants stood up and half remained sitting. The rabbi, learned as he was, did not know what to do. He consulted a house bound ninety-eight-year-old man who was the founder of their Temple. The rabbi

asked, "Is the tradition to stand during prayer?" The old man said, "No, that's not the tradition." The rabbi proceeded to ask, "Is the tradition to sit during *Shema*?" The old man answered, "No that's not the tradition, either." The rabbi cried, "But the congregants fight all the time, arguing whether they should sit or stand." The old man interrupted, exclaiming, "*That* is our tradition!"

The Saturday morning Torah crowd was small but stable. The same people participating in discussing the *Parasha* shared a meatless potluck meal in the study room. These events were typically followed by coffee and cake in one of the small cafes in downtown Zagreb. Although the importance of kosher food laws was a frequent topic among congregants, the apparent irony of negating kosher food laws (buying coffee and cake in a cafe on Saturday) marks the sociable nature of such gatherings. Torah study was not an insular occasion. Most congregants agreed that the reading and discussion of the *Parasha*, the meal and blessing of the wine, and the coffee with cake afterwards had become part of their Saturday rituals. But conforming to Jewish dietary laws in a strict sense was not an option for members. A *shohet* (a ritual slaughterer) was not available in Croatia at that time and neither were kosher products. Some members told me they had omitted pork from their diets while others, going a step further, made an attempt not to mix meat and dairy products.

The congregants exhibited a strong sense of Jewish religious identity. They were concerned with what they perceived to be the most authentic (Orthodox) practice of Judaism and insider status. According to one person's definition, one needed to make Judaism part of his or her everyday life and a personally relevant part of his or her overall life in order to gain insider status. The meaning of community and Jewish identity for these observant individuals found expression not only in attending services, but also through social interaction with others in things like shared meals. Ultimately, social interaction was at the center of the meaning of the Jewish community, understood as a commitment to a code of shared values that are malleable enough to accommodate individual expressions of Jewish culture, yet specific enough to contain feelings of group unity.

The divergent articulations of the Jewish community are exemplified through the social organization of the physical community. As we have seen, the changes in the ŽOZ interior over the last century reflect the changing meaning of Jewish community life and, perhaps more importantly, its will to survive despite all odds. Central to the rift of change and the survival of the Jewish community are questions about the community's orientation toward inclusion and exclusion. These tensions are exemplified in the traditionalist views, expressed by the religiously observant who seek to keep the Jewish community insulated from the society in which it is situated, and modern views, expressed by more outward-centered community members. The physical manifestations of these views were described in the differing uses of community space that reflect the deeper meaning of the Jewish community. These meanings range from using the ŽOZ space for recreation and maintenance of friendships, and education, to using it for religious observance.

## CONCLUSION

As the foregoing demonstrates, the identity of the Jewish community is encoded in the social organization of the physical space of the ŽOZ. Once guided by an evolving social crisis that resulted in helping those in need of humanitarian aid, activities offered outside these times have been marked by social interaction in response to a different kind of crisis: the crisis of Jewish identity. Indeed, the organization of the physical space plays an important *causal* role in accentuating the cultural identity of its members as well as the self-image of the community. This is evidenced by, among other things, the array of activities offered in the ŽOZ. In particular, the social organization of the different spaces within the ŽOZ facilitates social interaction among members, while providing them with the resources to express Jewish culture through participation in activities and events such as folkloric dance, ceramics, foreign language classes, and various programs organized by the *Miroslav Salom Freiberger* cultural society. The proliferation of opportunities for engaging in cultural activities has had the corresponding effect of positioning a sense of Jewish cultural identity at the center of the self-identity of many ŽOZ members. This arguably marks a shift away from more traditional versions of Jewish self-understanding, rooted in the ideals of social welfare and relief efforts.

Not all community members embrace this shift in emphasis, but most agree that the continuation of the Jewish community is the top priority. That said, opinions range on how to go about securing the survival of the community and what type of relations the community should sustain with the society with in which it coexists. In addition to changes in the social organization of the interior space of the ŽOZ, recent changes to the exterior of the building have played an equally important role in transforming the community's image. One particularly striking example of this is the effect of the increase in security. The continuous presence of armed security guards at the entrance to the building, as well as the metal detectors and surveillance cameras positioned just inside the foyer have made the *apćina* less welcoming to outsiders and has created a perception of the ŽOZ as an insular community. On the other hand, we have seen that the newly refurbished *klub* and the adjacent theater have made the *općina* more inviting to outsiders; in addition to marking a shift in the self-identity of the members of the ŽOZ toward a stronger sense of Jewish cultural identity, the availability of spaces within the community designated for participation in Jewish cultural events and activities has resulted in an increased interaction *between* community members and visitors.

Another change to the interior that has had a significant impact on the community is the recent construction of robust offices and a large conference room, all of which are located on the ground level. These spaces tend to legitimize the ŽOZ as giving them an official feel, while at the same time rendering the ŽOZ more inviting for prominent outsiders.

In the next chapter, I explore the differing views about the meaning of the ŽOZ and its spiritual leadership. In particular, I examine the conflict between traditionalist and humanist understanding of the ŽOZ by focusing on the arrival of the first community rabbi in Croatia since 1943 and the debates over the form and function of the future *Praška* space. I point out that both events have accentuated and brought into public debate the already existing tensions between traditionalists, who view the ŽOZ community as a place of worship, and the humanists who view the ŽOZ as a place in which the diverse expressions of Jewish identity within the community can be expressed.

## Chapter Four

# Forward and Back: The Traditionalist and Integrationist Debates

In 1940, when the Jewish community in Zagreb had eleven thousand members, the ŽOZ owned several buildings, including one synagogue and a sports club. After the Holocaust, when the communist regime was established, eleven out of twelve buildings previously owned by the ŽOZ became state property. All that remained between 1945 and 2003 was the building located on *Palmotićeva* (the current site of the ŽOZ). In 1992, during the so-called denationalization process, where property seized during communism was returned to its original owners, the community began negotiating the return of ŽOZ property through Croatian civil court. The most important space the community sought to reacquire was an empty lot in *Praška*—the former site of the only synagogue in Zagreb.

Built according to the designs of Franjo Klein, the synagogue was consecrated in 1867 and destroyed by the *Ustaša* government between November 1941 and the spring of 1942. The grand opening was a public event attended by many of Zagreb's residents, including the elite and professional classes. The papers were full of praise. Klein's synagogue was a creative interpretation of his inspiration, Ludwig Von Forester (a Viennese designer who built the first synagogue during the Hapsburg Monarchy). Klein's design was so impressive that it eventually became the prototype for synagogues in many other European cities (Knežević, 1998).

Another seminal event for the ŽOZ was the arrival of the community's permanent rabbi in 1998, the first since World War II. Croatia did not have a permanent rabbi since Miroslav Salom Freiberger was deported to Auschwitz in the spring of 1943. Since then, rabbis from neighboring Hungary and Israel visited Croatia during the High Holidays, a practice that continued until the appointment of Rabbi Kotel Danon.

Kotel, as ŽOZ members affectionately call him, is a young man in his early forties, born and educated in Israel (rabbinical school) and later in Hungary (law school), where he met his wife. When Kotel and his wife arrived in Zagreb in 1998, they had one small child. By 2004, they had four children, as is required under the Orthodox principles by which Kotel lives.

In the previous chapter, we saw the effects of identity politics, as played out in the *Palmotićeva* space. In this chapter, I focus on the conflict between traditionalist and integrationalist views of the potential future site of the ŽOZ in the *Praška* space. Through the narratives of ŽOZ members, I address two interrelated themes: the arrival of the community rabbi in 1998 and the conceptualization of the future of the ŽOZ through ideas about the organization of the *Praška* space. In particular, I focus on the conflicting views of the ŽOZ community by examining the direction of the ŽOZ's spiritual leadership and the debates over the form and function of the future *Praška* space.

## THE RABBI AND THE COMMUNITY

> We had been promised a rabbi for quite a while now. It felt like we had been waiting for the messiah to arrive and save our community, but when he finally came we felt disillusioned.

The ŽOZ commenced a search for a permanent rabbi sometime in the early 1990s. Visiting rabbis came from as far away as the United States starting in 1992. They usually stayed for a couple of days, a week at most. The search was arduous mainly because the members and the international support organizations that helped finance the rabbinic position disagreed about the right person for the job. For many ŽOZ members, it was as much a question of the rabbi's personality as about his denomination (Reform, Conservative, or Orthodox). For the international support organizations (whose motives I discuss in chapter 6) the most important criterion was the rabbi's denomination.

Some ŽOZ members were in favor of an Orthodox rabbi, reasoning that Orthodoxy would save the community from its demise. In their view, a reformed branch of Judaism would only lead members further away from living an *authentic* Jewish life. In contrast, many nonobservant members stressed that the presence of a rabbi would endow the community with a political identity and provide members, especially the young, with Jewish education. They saw the rabbi's function as social in the sense that a rabbi represents the ŽOZ to the outside world. For them, the rabbi's denomination was not the only determining factor.

Many candidates passed through the community before Kotel was inaugurated in the autumn of 1998. Prior to moving to Zagreb, Kotel had visited the

ŽOZ on several occasions throughout 1996–1997; he claimed that more people had become interested in Judaism since his visits.

I spoke with Rabbi Kotel in his comfortable office on the third floor of the ŽOZ, next to the library and down the hall from the small synagogue. The rabbi wore slacks and a sports coat; he sported a closely trimmed beard and a black, barely noticeable skullcap, the same color as his hair. He had a pleasant demeanor, and despite our language gap (I speak neither Hungarian nor Hebrew, and Kotel had mastered neither English nor Croatian) he had no difficulty communicating his goals for the future of the ŽOZ.

In my interview with him, he said that his role as the chief rabbi of Croatia is "not a political function." According to him, rabbis are not supposed to engage in political, or what he called "external," relations. (He did not believe that his visits to the Croatian parliament in 1998 and 1999 contradicted these views.) Despite being avowedly apolitical, Kotel brought the ŽOZ to the attention of the European rabbinical community and other international philanthropic Jewish organizations, all of which promised to sponsor religious projects as soon as the opportunity presented itself.

One such project was the configuration of the *Praška* space. The rabbi said that if the ŽOZ decided to build a synagogue on the *Praška* lot he would make sure to get sponsors for the project, but—he added during our conversation—if the community decided to build a community center and a smaller synagogue (as seems to be the current plan), then he would have nothing to do with the project.

When I asked Kotel about the future of the ŽOZ, he said that the greatest challenge for the future of Croatian Jews would be to bring the Jewish community back to the type of community the ŽOZ was before World War II. He believed that the best way to do this is to increase the number of converts, establish religious education programs, and to ensure the koshering of the ŽOZ. Conversion would have to be supervised by rabbinical judges (a number of judges from Israel agreed to come to Croatia if the community had at least six prospective converts). This is necessary, he explained, in order for the converted to be recognized by the State of Israel under rabbinical law. Kotel believed conversion to be a means of securing the survival of the Jewish community. Together with conversion, Kotel regarded religious education to be of foremost importance for the future of the ŽOZ community. His contacts with the international Orthodox community enabled him to send several ŽOZ members to Israel to obtain Jewish religious education. In 2000, four young people from the ŽOZ were enrolled in religious schools in Israel, paid for by philanthropists from the United States. The same organizations sponsored educational materials, including new Torahs, and the koshering of the ŽOZ.[1]

## THE ŽOZ: PLACE OF ENACTMENT OF JEWISH CULTURE OR COMMUNITY OF WORSHIP?

Because the rabbi's presence has impacted different aspects of community life, I asked members to talk about the need for a rabbi, conversion, religious education, and the koshering of the ŽOZ. I also asked them to talk about the future of the ŽOZ.

Some members believed that the ŽOZ does not need a rabbi because the community survived for so long without one. "The rabbi is probably the only fully religious person in our community," someone said. Another person boasted, "Who cares about the rabbi? Our lives go on with or without him." Surprisingly, some members who did not identify as observant Jews stressed the importance of an Orthodox rabbi. An Orthodox rabbi best "looked" the job they said. The reasoning behind this view was that such a person would be taken most seriously in matters outside of the ŽOZ community. These members reasoned that an Orthodox rabbi would be more credible on the international front and would be the best person to represent the ŽOZ in local and international matters.

But the majority of the community members I interviewed strongly believed that the ŽOZ needs a rabbi and that Jewish education is of utmost importance to the maintenance of the community, but they did not see conversion as crucial to the survival of the ŽOZ. After all, many described themselves as "citizens of the world" and "cultural Jews." They recognized the importance of a rabbi for the ŽOZ, even if they themselves were not particularly interested in religious observance. A rabbi's function was described most frequently as that of a "Jewish educator." Members stressed that a rabbi, in his role as educator, needed to be able to communicate with his students. In order to do that well, he should know the history of his community, speak the local language, and embrace the local culture and, most importantly, address the needs of the community. There was, however, little agreement about the right person for the position or his denomination, or even what Jewish education entails exactly. The following represents the dominant view:

> Our community needs a rabbi. Such a person must be the spiritual leader of the Jewish community. In a community with a history like ours, a rabbi not only conducts services, he informs people about Jewish traditions.

I asked three constituencies active in the ŽOZ about the role of the rabbi: those who identify as cultural Jews, those who identify as observant Jews, and the management. By far the most common belief about the role of the rabbi was that his presence would strengthen the image of the ŽOZ in Croatian society. This is how Illan, who identified as a "citizen of the world," put it:

> I have always been in favor of having a rabbi in this community. It is not that I need him, but without a rabbi we would not survive in a country like Croatia. Things were different in Yugoslavia. Today, a rabbi or priest is an expected standard in Croatia; without him we would be considered an illegitimate minority.

Tomislav, a humanistic Jew, expressed a similar view:

> This community needs a rabbi, that's for sure. In this part of the world, a rabbi ful-fills a political function. He represents our community to the outside world. If that was not the case, we would not need a rabbi and I would personally be against having a rabbi that cost our community a great deal of money.

The majority of the ŽOZ membership understood the rabbi's position as social in terms of Croatian national politics. The rabbi was not only viewed as the spiritual representative of the Jewish community but as an educator who could *inform* members about Jewish traditions. Ironically, Kotel, who understood his role only within the context of the ŽOZ and the wider Orthodox world, did not share these views. He saw himself as an educator only to the extent that he would be able to establish Jewish religious laws in the ŽOZ.

The majority view was also in conflict with the ŽOZ's observant or traditionalist minority, who were concerned about the return to what they perceived to be a more *authentic* expression of Jewish identity. They viewed the presence of an Orthodox rabbi as helping to facilitate such an image and helping them to lead an observant Jewish life. For the observant minority, the "return" to Orthodox practices really meant a reassembling of the new perceptions of Jewish identity.

From the management's perspective, one of the most important reasons for having a rabbi was the community's image. The presence of a rabbi was understood as legitimizing the Jewish community regardless of the different perceptions of his role in the community. The majority of the persons interviewed on this topic felt that a Reform rabbi would have been the best choice for the community: "An open person who can represent our community for what it really is and not what he thinks it should be."

Mirjana:
> I will tell you very openly, I am sorry that our rabbi is not a reformed rabbi but many say that it is good this way because otherwise the community would diminish. I do not have knowledge about this and I do not want to predict the future but I do know that more people would attend the seminars here if we had a more flexible rabbi.

Mira:
> I am not sure if our rabbi is the best choice for this community, but at the moment
> we do not have anybody else. Basically, we need someone who would be able to
> adjust to the needs of our community and who fits in with our mentality. We also
> need a rabbi because our children need to have a Jewish education. Without Jewish
> education they will receive Catholic education in school or they will have nothing.

Zvonko:
> I think that the best person for this place is someone who emotionally and intellectu-
> ally fits into our community. Such a rabbi would be ideal for us. I would like to see
> someone who is from here and who understands our people. I think that it would be
> necessary if not indispensable for us to have a rabbi who is from Zagreb, or at the
> very least from Croatia. It is important that he understands our problems and that he
> speaks Croatian, because practically nobody understands the prayers in Hebrew. I
> think that it is important to have the prayers in Croatian and Hebrew, not only in
> Hebrew. In the past there was always one part [of the prayers] that was spoken in
> Croatian so that the people who do not understand Hebrew could participate.

Members recognized the importance of a rabbi for the community in terms
of Jewish education for the children, but felt at the same time that the current
rabbi is too conservative, too costly, and may potentially turn people away
from the community. The overall sentiment was that the rabbi is inflexible
about the needs of the community and has had a hard time adjusting.

Vesna, who is committed to Orthodox Judaism, offered a different view on
the role and performance of the rabbi:

> I think that our rabbi needs to be regarded as our way out of assimilation. He is
> someone who could, if we open ourselves to the possibility, expand our very poor
> knowledge of Judaism. He is our only hope for survival. Our poor rabbi initially
> experienced a shock when he came to our community because we don't know what
> it means to be Jews anymore. He could not believe what is done here. But he stayed
> and made many positive changes, including organizing the elementary school and
> learning to speak Croatian.

Ultimately, members were mostly concerned about the strictness of Orthodoxy and not the rabbi as an individual. Many said they liked Rabbi Kotel.
They thought of him as a nice and kind man. But they were concerned that
he would change the image of the *općina* too much; they preferred to keep
the *općina* the way it was before the rabbi implemented the religious laws.
They also feared that Orthodoxy could make the rabbi decide that all ŽOZ
members must formally convert to Judaism and become *Halachic* Jews
(according to Jewish law) as a condition of membership. Such demands could
exclude many people and thereby change the image of the community from
a predominantly secular and inclusive place, where Jewish culture is enacted,

to an exclusive community of worship. In my view, members tended to overestimate the rabbi's power and influence over the community, but perceptions ranged from the view that Orthodoxy may destroy the community to the view that it would save it. Skeptical about the arrival of a rabbi, Duško offered a more long-term view:

> There have been five hundred rabbis through here. This one is no different from any other. He will tell his story, collect his money, and move on. We will wait for the next rabbi and the next one, and in the meantime our lives go on. He affects our lives very little.

A rabbi's role was very clearly perceived as important in terms of Jewish education for children. I asked Mirjana what she thought about the role of new rabbi. She replied, "People need to know about Jewish culture before they could even appreciate a rabbi." She explained,

> I don't go to synagogue because I'm just not that type of a person, but I think without any doubt that we need to have a rabbi here because we need someone to represent our own community and identity. Considering that we now live in a Catholic country where priests and nuns in school teach subjects to children, we need to have different opportunities for religious education for our children. If we don't do that, they will become Catholics or worse: nothing. So, basically we need to have something that is ours. And we need to cherish this. The rabbi's function is to educate our young, represent our community to the outside world, and provide an opportunity to those people who want to be involved in the community on a religious level. As for me personally, the rabbi's presence neither interferes nor adds to my life here.

According to Dragan, a rabbi is needed in the community because "most people do not know what it means to be Jewish. A rabbi should be in charge of Jewish education, which our community desperately needs." He also pointed out that "our community needs someone to teach us about Jewish history and religion, but we don't need doctrine."

Darko was convinced that the arrival of the rabbi would enable non-Jewish Croatians to become more informed about Croatian Jews. Darko's comment backfired shortly after his remark. In an interview with a local newspaper, Kotel proclaimed that he wanted to have a *mikvah* (a ritual bathhouse used mostly by ultra Orthodox Jews) installed at the *općina*. Unfamiliar with Jewish religious practices, the article depicted the community as backward and involved in curious rituals. Many people in the ŽOZ were outraged by the rabbi's comments. Further misunderstanding grew when the rabbi declined to attend a function sponsored by the Ministry of Culture because Jewish law forbade him from entering a church. The following was a common response to his actions:

I think that any person living in an environment like ours has to be a diplomat. He has to cooperate with other religious communities in Croatia. I think that the most important part of his job is representing our community to the outside world. He has not done this successfully. I recall an event organized at some church in Opatovina, to which the rabbi was invited. Not only did he not attend the event as the representative of our community, he sent a group of dancers instead.

I was told that the management began curtailing the rabbi's public speaking events due to the management's fear that negative depictions of the ŽOZ and the rabbi would result in anti-Semitism. Further misunderstandings arose when the rabbi began implementing religious burial rites in the ŽOZ. I heard from several people informally that the rabbi was not able to grant their loved one a Jewish funeral if the deceased had not been a *Halachic* Jew or if the family members desired an ecumenical funeral, in accordance with the wishes of the deceased. The rabbi was willing to overlook the *Halachic* part in the case of administering funerals for intercultural Jews, but he would not compromise on the presence of non-Jewish religious themes at the funeral (e.g., the presence of a Catholic priest or having the funeral procession begin in one of the small chapels installed at the Mirogoj Cemetery). Kotel was neither idiosyncratic nor ethnocentric about his views; he was simply following frequently misunderstood Orthodox practice. Here is how one member interpreted his actions:

You would not believe how upset we all were when [the rabbi] denied my friend's husband a Jewish funeral. He was a Catholic and supposedly religious. According to him she could not even go to her husband's funeral. The whole thing was very painful because her husband had been a member of our community for many years already, and they had both been coming to services on Friday nights!

Finally, I asked participants whether the ŽOZ community should have a rabbi or whether a *madricha* would be sufficient. This is what one of the young women, who teaches in the newly established Jewish school, said:

I think that both of them are important for our community. Our community was always active, even without a rabbi, but the rabbi helped us in many ways to connect with Jewish traditions that were long forgotten here. He even helped me personally because I would not have been able to study in Israel without him. I doubt that somebody would either have those kinds of connections or help organize the young people and provide those opportunities for them. In the past, the Jewish school was just something people would talk about, but he made the school a reality. When it comes to *madrachim*, I think that it is important for the children to have someone they can relate to. I think that it is always easier to listen to somebody in their twenties, who has some knowledge about Jewish culture and some life experience, than someone in their fifties.

The turmoil also arose during the koshering of the ŽOZ. As soon as his appointment began, the rabbi made sure that the ŽOZ kitchen was kosher. Part of the koshering process involved having a Jewish person handle all food prepared and sold at the *općina*. A *Halachic* Jew was hired for this task. When possible, kosher foods were imported from neighboring Hungary; otherwise, fresh fruits and vegetables were used. Currently, the kitchen is as kosher as local products and the implementation of religious laws allow it to be. Differently put, since there are few *Halachic* Jews in Croatia and no *shohet*, koshering of the the ŽOZ has been only possible to an extent. The real kosher controversy began when Maria, a woman who had previously worked at the kitchen adjacent to the *klub* and who was not Jewish, was no longer needed. Rumors had it that Kotel had Maria, a Croat, fired because of the implementation of kosher laws. In contrast, members from the observant group insisted that the claim was ridiculous and that Maria had left on her own accord. Everyone had something to say about the kosher kitchen. Either the food was not as good anymore, or it tasted much better because it was kosher. In a sense everybody's expectations about koshering were very high. Andrea insisted that, while she might be eating pork outside the *općina*, people needed to pay respect to Jewish laws in the ŽOZ:

> When the rabbi came, the kosher kitchen was started. This disturbed many people. We asked ourselves, Why do we need a kosher kitchen? We have lived for sixty years without it. Why do we need this nonsense now? To be fair, not everybody in the community thought about it like I do. Some were happy about everything being kosher even though they don't eat kosher at home. In the end, I think that it is OK to have a kosher environment inside these walls. Ultimately, we can do whatever we want outside these walls.

Many other members were not as accepting as Andrea. They wanted to learn about Jewish traditions and history without the religious doctrine they perceived as backward. Not being able to come and go as they pleased and eat what they wanted (members were used to preparing homemade dishes for the Family Sabbath) was upsetting and disorienting. The monthly Family Sabbath is an example of the type of discord I witnessed. Prior to Kotel's arrival, the Family Sabbath was a lively event. Nicola held a short service for the few (often less than ten) interested observers before joining the lively crowd for a communal potluck meal in the *klub*. A variety of dishes were brought to these events. Senior women prepared the dishes several days beforehand and shared recipes with others. The Family Shabbat attracted between forty and seventy people prior to Kotel's arrival. Since 1998 the event has changed dramatically. .Since the food has to be kosher, the ŽOZ now supplies all the food that is prepared in the kosher kitchen. Members are no longer able to bring homemade dishes to the Family Shabbat. Moreover, they are encouraged to pay a small fee in order to participate. The services, conducted by Kotel, are much longer and continue in the *klub* prior to the commencement of the Shabbat meal. Many consultants complained that the rabbi's prayers and lectures went on too long (a forty-five minute performance was not out of the ordinary). During this time, members had to sit still and listen to the rabbi before they could begin their meal. I was sitting next to Ruth, a Holocaust survivor who is hearing impaired, during one of these sermons. She said loud and clear for the whole room to hear: "What is he talking about? Why can't we eat already?" Ruth was worried that she would not be able to make it to the bus in the dark by herself if the dinner lasted too long. Other members observed that it was no longer fun to come to the Family Shabbat since, according to Darko, the rabbi "always goes on and on and we can't understand what he says." Darko's observation was about Kotel's Croatian language skills. Here is what another retiree had to say:

> I think that there are many people, especially of my generation, who no longer come to the community because of the rabbi. We were not brought up in a religious way, but now that we have a rabbi, we cannot come here and do whatever we want. On Friday afternoon, he insists on having the *klub* closed. He also insists on the ceremonial hand washing [ritual during services], something we are not familiar with. Some adopted the Orthodox way and that is of course their right. But most of us feel uncomfortable with all the strict rules he imposes. I think that we should have had somebody who could introduce us to the cultural milieu of Judaism, not to Jewish doctrine. I know for a fact that most Israelis don't keep to those rules. I do not know how many people he bothers because I do not have the numbers. But I do know that many people from my generation [who grew up in Yugoslavia] do not come here anymore because they feel that things are no longer the way they used to be.

A younger member presented similar concerns:

> Since the rabbi started coming to the youth meeting I started coming less and less. I think that it is OK that we have a rabbi, but I think that it would be great if we had somebody who is from here [Croatia] and a member of our community. That would be much simpler than what we have now, a man from a different country who does not have much in common with our tradition or the history of this community. Another problem is that he does not speak Croatian. It would be great to have a person such as Rabbi Isak Asijel from Belgrade, who is Orthodox and at the same time very flexible, precisely because he knows the history of this community and knows that with a strictly religious and conservative program the community would become divided. I think that people back away from such strictness [in Croatia and Yugoslavia] and that only a smaller number lean towards it. It seems to me that that is precisely what happened here. Only a very small minority of the people here are religious, and only they are pleased with the rabbi.

# DELIBERATIONS CONCERNING
## THE *PRAŠKA* SPACE

Although little documentation survived, an exhibition about the *Praška* syna-gogue entitled "Zagreb's Synagogue—*Reliquiae Reliquiarum*," or the rem-nant of the remnants was held at a downtown art gallery in 1997. The exhibit displayed the remaining few photographs (dating back to 1881) that mark the building's impressive façade and interior decor. The exhibition was an hom-age to a bygone era, taking spectators back to Zagreb in the latter part of the nineteenth century. The photographs were presented as a document of Zagrebian architecture, urban geography, and cultural life. They were as much, if not more, about Zagreb in the 1880s as they were a representation of Jewish life. The use of the Latin phrase, *Reliquiae Reliquiarum*, instead of the Hebrew equivalent, *she'erit hashe'eriyot*, is emblematic of the accultu-rated character of the Jewish community. By using the Latin phrase the exhibit sought to communicate a sense of familiarity to the wider (Roman Catholic) public. Using the Hebrew equivalent would have emphasized Jew-ish "otherness" if not "foreignness," a message that the ŽOZ was trying to avoid during the xenophobic Tuđman era.

Even more memorable than *Reliquiae Reliquiarum* photographs of the *Praška* synagogue was the virtual reconstruction of the synagogue created by architects Ivana and Tomislav Kušan a year earlier in 1996. Their digital simulation shows the synagogue in a modern background. The artists super-imposed an image of the actual synagogue taken from the remaining photo-graphs onto photographs taken of the present-day environment. In the composite the synagogue occupies what is today a parking lot. Its gray struc-ture (the image was taken from a black and white photograph) stands next to ivory and light blue buildings. The foreground is filled with cars and people, including a young redheaded woman with a baby stroller. The photograph captures the moment at which she turns her head to face what she sees as an empty lot and what the viewer sees as the grand synagogue. Ognjen Kraus, president of the ŽOZ, described the simulation as follows:

> The computer reconstruction has a twofold function: a recreation of a monument to Jewish life in Zagreb, and a renewal of memories of it. The exhibition is a stage in our extensive work on Zagreb and Croatia's Jewish heritage. The Croatian Jewish communities will use all their resources to continue this work with the help of those who consider this heritage an integral part of the cultural heritage of the Republic of Croatia. For the Jewish community, it is a debt paid to their identity and tradition, to those who disappeared in the Holocaust, and to those who went before them. In the near future, I believe we shall succeed in our plans to build a memorial syna-gogue and a museum. We intend to build it on the site of the old synagogue, as part

of a multifunctional center that will once more embellish the place of our memories (Knežević, 1998).

Architects Ivana and Tomislav Kušan, in a recently published commentary on the digital reconstruction of the synagogue, said that the surviving architectural plans do not provide enough information to reconstruct the building as designer Klein intended it. The interior would be particularly difficult to replicate because not enough information about the building has survived. Moreover, they opined that once the property was returned to the Jewish community, the community would be better served by commissioning a new design, one that would serve to memorialize the synagogue while at the same time responding to the present-day needs of the community. The Kušans suggested organizing an international competition of architects to fulfill those goals.

Three years after the exhibit, in December 1999, the property was finally returned to the community through the denationalization proceedings. In December 2001, another exhibition entitled "Synagogue and Zagreb" was installed in the city's Archeological Museum. Rather than a document of a bygone era, this exhibition focused on the meaning of the synagogue in Zagreb in the twentieth century through visual and written testimonies. One of its main purposes was to foster public interest in the reconstruction of the *Praška* space while educating the public about the fate of Croatian Jews during the Holocaust. The exhibition made the point that the synagogue had been the exemplary symbol of Jewish presence and history in the city of Zagreb. Its central location and prominent architectural style was a constant reminder of the city's minority population. In the spirit of documenting the destruction of the Jewish people and their material culture the synagogue's destruction was documented on film. This visual recording was presented at the exhibition through an excerpt of the film *Zagreb's Synagogue—1876–1941* which served as a reminder of the atrocities committed by the *Ustaša* regime at the time of the synagogue's destruction. The excerpt (only one minute of the recording of the destruction was preserved) was shown on a big screen without sound.

The exhibition also sought to inform the public about the process of *Praška's* return to the Jewish community in 2000 and the resulting dialogue about the future of the *Praška* space. Its return to the Jewish community did not come without a struggle. Since 1945, *Praška* had housed a number of commercial venues, including a parking lot. Over the years, plans for a shopping mall and business headquarters have been proposed but none have been realized. Then, in 1986, at the time when the ŽOZ began changing its self-image, plans for a memorial synagogue and cultural center began to be articulated. Although the war in Yugoslavia delayed the realization of the *Praška* project, it has continued to be the subject of debate and study of ŽOZ members and Zagreb residents, including architecture students from Zagreb University.

Prominent Jewish community members and public figures from Zagreb were asked about the future of *Praška*. The questionnaire aimed to solicit views about the reconstruction of the exterior as well as the interior of the building (Kovač, 2002). Views about the purpose of the building ranged from those who wished to see the building used strictly for the purpose of religious observance to those favoring a multipurpose use of the space. Similarly, views about the exterior design of the building ranged from those who wanted a replica of the synagogue to those who preferred a building that would embrace the contemporary spirit of the community. The compromise plan, believed to guarantee international funding, was to build a replica of the façade and an adaptation of the interior that would fit the needs of the current community. The replica of the façade would serve to memorialize the importance of the synagogue. Perhaps more importantly, it would serve as a public reminder of the events that took place in Croatia from 1941 to 1945.

Ivo Goldstein (Kovač, 2002) argued that the replica of the façade would serve to assert that the Jewish community in Croatia continues to exist despite all odds:

> This generation did not buy this property; it inherited it from the generation that disappeared in the Holocaust. Our generation is not completely free to do what it wants with this space. We do not have the right to experiment on the site of vandalism. Why did the *Ustašas* destroy the synagogue and not the [community center] building in *Palmotićeva* or the *Lavoslav Schwarts* [Jewish nursing home] in *Maksimirska*? They destroyed it because it was one of the symbols of the city and the Jewish community for three-quarters of a century. The destruction of the synagogue was supposed to be the symbol of the destruction of the Jewish community in Zagreb. The erection of the replica at the beginning of the 21st century should show that the Jewish community still exists. The building is a part of the logo of the Jewish Community to this day, and it remains a symbol of the local Jewry.

The promise of funding from outside the Jewish community was expressed by a number of unexpected sources, all of whom agreed that the exterior should be a replica of the destroyed synagogue and that the building should solely house a synagogue. The archbishop of Zagreb expressed the·view that the most appropriate uses of the property would be in accordance with the needs of its religious practitioners. Similarly, the president of the Islamic community in Zagreb, promised to provide financial aid to the *Praška* project in the event that the Jewish community reached the decision to rebuild

Klein's synagogue. He stated furthermore that he had the opportunity to view photographs of the synagogue, which impressed him because it was the only Moorish style building at that time and would, had it not been destroyed, represent extraordinary architectural value to Zagreb. Examined historically, these views are curious since, as we have already seen in previous chapters, the architectural features of the building reflect the relativist worldview of the majority of its community members. Recall that Orthodox Jews, who refused to participate in services held at *Praška* along with the non-Orthodox, rented their own space.

Not everyone who was reverent about preserving the style and function of the building felt that the replica needed to be viewed as solely a place for religious observance. Some believed that a replica synagogue would serve in itself as a memorial that could "rehabilitate the urban character" of the city. Opinions were expressed about the cultural and historical significance of having a Jewish place of worship in the center of town. On this view, the building was envisioned as a place of memory and history. It could serve as a cultural-informational center that could nourish Jewish tradition and solidify social relations with interested visitors. One observer felt that replicating Klein's synagogue is something that the residents of Zagreb owe to the urban history of Zagreb, the Jewish community, and to "our common memory." He maintained that

> the synagogue in *Praška* is one of the signs of the cultural progress of Zagreb in the middle of nineteenth century. The building of the synagogue was a monument that bore evidence to the multicultural reality of Zagreb. The fact that we had a Catholic cathedral, synagogue, Orthodox, and Protestant church in the center of the city, is one of the important indicators of Zagreb's highly developed urban character and cultural tolerance which existed in the nineteenth century.

Perhaps predictably, a dignitary from the Croatian academy of arts and sciences stated that the *Praška* building should be modern and architecturally noteworthy. The building should incorporate a memorial and religious section and have a multipurpose culture center. On this view, the best way to accomplish these goals would be by organizing an international competition for architectural design. The architectural project should ideally connect the community's past, present, and future.

## WHEN STYLE DOES NOT FOLLOW FUNCTION: THE FUTURE OF THE *PRAŠKA* SPACE

The question of the function and organization of the *Praška* space is a crucible for the larger public debate about the meaning of the Jewish community and its political significance, governance, and continuation. Therefore, in order to elicit the diversity of views pertaining to Jewish identity and community life, I asked consultants (ordinary community members, not prominent community members, residents, or public figures) to describe what they would like to see built in the *Praška* lot. I asked them to imagine how they would engineer and plan the use of the space. What should the space hold? A synagogue replacing the one that was destroyed in 1942? A memorial synagogue in addition to a museum, as Kraus suggested? And, if so, what would they like to see in the museum?

In contrast of the majority of the prominent and public voices on the topic, many consultants shared the view that the space and the actual design of the building should not be a replica of the one destroyed in 1942, either in its form or function. In other words, the building should not only be used as a synagogue. Consultants felt that in addition to a space dedicated to a synagogue, the building should also incorporate a museum. Different opinions about the thematic content of the museum were expressed. In some instances, the museum was envisioned as a place that could potentially attract the wider public and educate them about, for example, Croatia's role during the Holocaust and the lives of Croatian Jews. Others viewed the museum as a place to display artifacts related to the wider Jewish world and the contributions of individual Jews in Croatian society. On this view, the community needed to be represented in a "realistic way" (i.e., as what it is and not on the basis of an idealized version of what a Jewish community ought to be). Consultants thought the most important themes a museum could address were the Holocaust, Judaism, and Jewish traditions in Croatia. Consultants stressed the importance of not presenting the Jewish community in Croatia as an isolated or exotic entity but rather as a modern community that is firmly rooted in Croatian society and the memory of the Holocaust:

> It would be much better to reconstruct the spirit of the building than to build a facsimile of the one that once existed. The synagogue was designed in accordance with the needs of our community at the time. It represented the architectural style of the time and was without doubt one of the more important architectural monuments of our city. The new building ought to once again respond to our needs and the needs of the residents of Zagreb. We have never been a very religious community. Our community is therefore better served if it incorporates a small synagogue and museum as a memorial of the past instead of building a synagogue for the fifteen or so individuals who attend services regularly. The center should contain a library, kosher restaurant, and museum. There definitely needs to be a museum in addition to anything else they are going to decide on. I think that the museum part should not be up for debate. The museum should focus on how this community went through a variety of changes and what it has become today. The museum should not only represent the past but also the present and the future.

The view expresses the array of ideological discourses about the meaning of identity and community, situated somewhere between a spiritual universe and the experience of everyday life. It also exemplifies how meaning and memory can be created through the museum. The importance of building a synagogue (small or larger) in *Praška* is closely related to the memory and negation of the fate of the Jewish community during the Holocaust. According to some consultants, rebuilding the synagogue means eulogizing the Jews who were killed in the Holocaust. The rebuilding of the synagogue, in whatever form, could potentially function as the most visible icon of Jewish survival in Croatia. The building of the synagogue is therefore strongly associated with the slogan "Never Again" and a sense of renewal, overcoming, and continuity. Consultants stressed that the atrocities committed against the Jews and the destruction of the synagogue should not be forgotten, but memorialized in the museum:

> I think that there are a lot of possibilities. The space downstairs should be like some sort of sacred place dedicated to remembrance. It could be like the Jewish museum in Prague. We could show a video with survivors talking about their experiences. We could also display objects that are related to the Holocaust in Croatia. I think that the most important reason for the museum is for the public to remember what happened here and not to think that the Holocaust did not happen in Croatia. Art objects are certainly very important, but there is no question when it comes to the history of Jews that the Holocaust needs to be addressed.

Consultants also emphasized that the conceptualization of *Praška* is not only for the purposes of it being a memorial, but also for representing the Jewish community for what it is. Here is another example:

> Basically, the center should represent our community in a realistic way. I would like it to be a living-teaching museum in addition to a cultural center and synagogue. I envision the museum more like a documentation center than an actual museum, where the people would find out about the history of the Jews, especially in this area. The exhibit should not only be about the history of Judaism, not that that is not important, but it should focus on all that has happened here in Croatia. The museum should be in part a dedication to the achievements of historic and living Croatian Jews. After all, our community is rich in personalities: we have writers, philosophers, mathematicians, lawyers, as well as *Ustaša* sympathizers.

The fact that many consultants expressed different activities they would like to see housed in the *Praška* space illustrates once again a sense of renewal and a focus on the future of Jewish community life. No one, to my knowledge, viewed *Praška* as solely a memorial space, but rather it was seen as a place for community members, interested residents of Zagreb, and cultural heritage tourists. The future center was envisioned as a lively, urban, and cosmopolitan gathering place revering the memory of the past and contributing to the creation of the community's future.

In the June 2004 issue of the ŽOZ's magazine *HA-kol* (meaning "all" or entire" in Hebrew), the community was informed that decisions about the financial and social organization and the purpose of the space would be made by an elected group of ŽOZ community representatives. At the time of this writing, deliberations about the organization of both the interior and the exterior of the building continue, including discussions about incorporating a synagogue, memorial space and wall of remembrance, an area for cultural activities, and an underground garage that would enable the community to generate funds necessary for its financial independence. Rumor has it that the entire ŽOZ may be moved to the new *Praška* space. The current space in the *Palmotićeva* would be rented or used as office space. With that in mind, the proposed uses of the *Praška* space—the parking garage and cultural center, in particular—remain in dispute. However, community representatives agree that it is Croatia's responsibility to help finance the building in order to come to terms with the powers that be that caused the demolition of the *Praška* synagogue. Ivo Sanader, the president of Croatia, and Vlasta Pavić, the mayor of Zagreb, have agreed to use government funds to help finance the construction of the building.

## CONCLUSION

While community members seldom agreed about the role and denomination of the rabbi, there was consensus that a rabbi was needed to secure the survival of the ŽOZ. Disagreement therefore focused on just how this was to be accomplished. The promotion of endogamy and the implementation of Jewish religious laws by the rabbi were perceived by the majority as "internalizing" enterprises—ones that would further alienate the ŽOZ community from Croatian society. Integrationists expressed concern that the exclusion of Croatian Jews from mainstream society would create a Jewish ghetto.

The majority of the ŽOZ community understood the rabbi's position as primarily social—that is, cooperating with Croatian political and religious leaders, and educating Croatian Jews about Jewish history and cultural traditions. As such, members' views conflicted with those of the rabbi and with traditionalists, who understood the rabbi's role as properly limited to religious education and the wider Orthodox world. Notably, the rabbi understood his social role as that of a mediator between the Orthodox Jewish world and the ŽOZ. Differences about the role of the rabbi notwithstanding, few members felt that the rabbi controlled the meaning of Jewish community life. Most members felt that their lives at the ŽOZ would continue to be meaningful regardless of the views of the rabbi. Indeed, many felt that the future of the ŽOZ had more to do with the future *Praška* site than the long-term goals of the rabbi.

For these individuals, the *Praška* space holds the promise of releasing the community from various obligations to the Croatian government and Jewish international aid. By developing an underground parking garage and commercial office space that could generate income, the *Praška* space could render the ŽOZ less financially dependent on local government agencies and international Jewish support organizations. Integrationists therefore advocate the multipurpose use of the *Praška* space, including a revenue-generating venture. This progressive and cosmopolitan view of the Jewish community is linked to humanist ideologies as well as to a concern with Croatian politics and free market enterprise. Such plans, however, are at odds with traditionalists, who advocate an isolationist view of the Jewish community and are more concerned with resurrecting the form and function of Klein's synagogue than financial independence.

Traditionalists insist on nothing short of a complete replica of the destroyed synagogue; they view the construction of the *Praška* space as being for the sole purpose of religious observance. The traditionalists emphasize an *authentic* notion of Jewish identity, as achieved through observance of Orthodox Judaism and a return to stable and predictable notions of community that in some ways shun the outside world. We have already seen an example of this in terms of the traditionalist nostalgia for kosher products. Beliefs such as these, interpreted anthropologically, bring out the features of a cultural system. That is, they do not merely signify the consumption of Jewish foods or synagogue design, but the consumption of material culture associated with ideology and identity.

Some local outsiders side with the traditionalists, arguing that the *Praška* space should be used only for religious purposes. Others go further than even the integrationists, insisting that the *Praška* building should be modern and architecturally noteworthy. According to this view, epitomized by the suggestion of an international competition for selecting the appropriate architect, the *Praška* space should serve not only to attract the attention of Zagrebians but also to connect the community's past, present, and future.

Tensions about the social and political roles that the rabbi and the *Praška* space could play also reflect ideas about the inward- and outward-centeredness of the Jewish community. Critics of eye-catching architecture and ornate interiors have described the nontraditionalist plans for the synagogue as too "outward-centered." Memories of the way things "used to be" and "used to look" and "ought to be and look" continue to play an important role in refashioning ideas about the future of the Jewish community in Croatia. The importance of the past reflects a vision of the Jewish community that is strongly associated with its continuation. For some, the future of the Jewish Croatian community is about the continuing integration of Jews into the new Croatian democracy and the multifaceted expression of Jewish identity. For others, the Jewish community is envisioned as a site for the negation of loss. That said, the diversity of views in the ŽOZ community share an interest in preserving the continuation of the Jewish community. They are divided by disagreement over the means for obtaining this and its meaning.

In the next chapter, I explore the newer meanings of Jewish identity through the lived experiences of ŽOZ members and, particularly, the interest shared by many ŽOZ members in connecting with their cultural heritage. Several factors that reveal the intercultural reality of Croatian Jews are discussed, including ideas about cultural signifiers, such as family names, and the process of discovering one's Jewish cultural background as an adult. I examine the motivations for such individuals to self define as Jews by pointing out that the process of identity renegotiation is at times dependent upon symbolic essentialism. Furthermore, I argue that these motivations are informed by sociopolitical factors, including the backlash of xenophobia experienced during Tuđman's Croatia, the disintegration of Yugoslavia (an experience many described as alienating), and the more attractive option for intercultural Jews of associating themselves with the Jewish community.

## NOTES

1. The koshering of a space is an extremely involved procedure. I have no information about how involved the ŽOZ was in helping to facilitate the process. At the very least all the equipment used needs to be cleaned to the point that no food or product residue, rust, or other materials can be detected. After sitting idle for a day and being inspected by the rabbi or a certified person, the food processing equipment has to be immersed in either liquid or dry heat.

## Chapter Five

# Who's Jewish, and Who Gets to Decide?

Most of my friends are from the [Jewish] community. All of them have a Jewish background, but there are differences between them if we look at [Jewish identity] in a strict sense of the definition. If a Jew is someone whose mother is Jewish, then I am already not a Jew. Yet I cannot be a Croat. Even if I wanted to, they would not accept me. So, I have [a sense of] renewed survival because I feel more like a Jew.

Mirna was one of my students in the English conversation class. She made this statement as we chitchatted before class one day. I asked her to write it down. Her statement exhibits her perceived biogenetic tie to the Jewish people and the sense in which her newfound Jewish identity—an identity she developed during the disintegration of Yugoslavia—was based upon symbolic essentialism. Recall that symbolic essentialism describes a useful strategy for individuals who are not able to trace their Jewish heritage back to their immediate families, but who nevertheless became vulnerable to discrimination during the transformation of the Yugoslav nation-state.

In 1991, when Mirna was no longer able to identify as Yugoslav, she discovered that having a Croat identity was not a viable option for her due to her Serbian and Jewish background. The latter derives from her paternal grandfather.

Mirna's newfound identity can be understood as a powerful strategy for dealing with the rapidly changing meaning of nationality and ethnicity in Yugoslavia at the time. She was convinced that identifying as a Jew was a better option than acknowledging her Serbian background, at a time when Croatia was at war with Yugoslavia, even though she and others like her were looked upon with suspicion and labeled as *novo-komponirani Židovi* (newly composed Jews) by ŽOZ skeptics.

As I learned from our conversation, Mirna's parents are neither Jewish by birth nor by self-identification. Mirna imagines her connectedness and her *innate sense of belonging* to the Jewish people as tied to her grandfather, a person she never knew who perished in the Holocaust. In order to overcome her feelings of inadequacy, she began expressing her Jewish identity through strict religious observance, projecting her view that *authentic* Jews are those who lead a pious life. Above all, Jewish identity for Mirna is about the "discovery of a beautiful tradition which is part of me."

In this chapter, I discuss how and why intercultural Jews such as Mirna choose to define themselves as Jews. I explore the interest shared by many ŽOZ members in connecting with their cultural heritage and with the newer meanings of Jewish identity. I consider several factors that presuppose the meaning of Jewish identity and point out that the process of identity negotiation is neither static nor determined by birth, but rather dependent upon symbolic essentialism. As the narratives of the ŽOZ members reveal, Jewish identity is contingent throughout an individual's lifetime and is therefore continually subject to environmental (social and political) as well as personal change.

In previous chapters, we have seen that identity transformations are traceable to the cultural politics of a particular place and time. Here, I explore the possibility that identity transformations are constructed in response to personal predilections and the intercultural reality of Croatian Jews. I do this by discussing several aspects of the lived experiences of intercultural Croatian Jews that reveal these predilections, including the discovery of a person's Jewish background in adulthood, and ideas about cultural signifiers, like family name and physical appearance.

## NEW DISCOVERIES: ADULTS CONNECTING WITH HIDDEN JEWISH PASTS

*Andrea*

Andrea is a twenty-something physics student. I met her in ceramics class, where we shared many laughs and cookies made by her grandmother (who lives with her and her parents). Andrea told me many details about the young men she was dating. We talked candidly about school and everyday life. When I asked Andrea if she would like to tell me about her parents' background (a routine question I posed in all of my interviews), she looked at me for a long time without saying anything. Her eyes were wide and clear: it was as if she wanted to respond, but the words would not come out. This was hardly the Andrea I knew from ceramics group. Talking about her parents' past was painful and evidently a taboo topic. It was the key to her private life—a life she previously thought to understand. This is what she finally told me:

> The first time I came [to the ŽOZ] was with a friend of mine who used to belong to the community. I was seventeen years old at the time. I remember it because I was still in the gymnasium. I think it was my last year. I never knew about the community before that time. My parents raised me as a non-Jew because they suffered a great deal during the war. Both my mom and dad lost their entire families. Many of them were taken to concentration camps, where they died. Mom survived by accident because she was not home at the time that her family was taken. She was out shopping, I think. When she came back, a neighbor told her not to go near her house. When she finally did go home, she found her house empty. Her entire family had been taken away. Dad survived because he ended up joining the Partisans. He hid in a forest with two of his brothers. The three of them survived. There were thirteen members of his family. Everybody except the three brothers was killed in the war. They were saved by having joined the Partisans. Because my parents had suffered so many traumas in their own families, they decided that the identities of their own children should remain hidden to outsiders. They were both from very religious families. But after the war they felt that "if God could let this happen, we do not want to have anything else to do with this God." And so they took us, my brother and me, away from God and religion completely.

Not wanting to invoke memories of the Holocaust was one of the main reasons parents gave for hiding their cultural background from their children. Another reason was loyalty to the ideals of Yugoslavia and to the Partisans, the resistance movement led by Tito from 1942 to 1945. After the war, during Tito's Yugoslavia, allegiance to any cultural group (ethnic or religious) meant the betrayal of *Yugoslavism*. Communist rhetoric, I was told in my interviews, discouraged the emphasis of cultural group identification, as this was perceived to detract from a larger sense of Brotherhood and Unity.

The force of this rhetoric explains why Andrea did not discover her mother's Jewish background until she was seventeen. Her mother, an active former Communist Party member, did not discuss her background or even mention the Holocaust to her daughter. Andrea never met her parents' siblings, who survived the Holocaust but died before Andrea was born. In fact, she had no information about anyone on either her mother's or father's side of the family.

Growing up, Andrea remembers her parents identifying primarily as communists and as atheists. Ethnicity and religion were, if mentioned at all, usually discussed in derogatory terms. Andrea's parents insisted that with the exception of adherence to *Yugoslavism*, cultural group identification would lead to separatism and nationalism, the twin ideological enemies of Brotherhood and Unity and the communist state. Similarly, organized religion was

understood to be hostile to state ideology and practiced only by the emotionally unstable, the backward and the superstitious. If communism was associated with modernity, the future, and a better, more equal world, religious
doctrine was associated with the Dark Ages, and an irrational and backward-
looking world.

But as the political system changed and Yugoslavia disintegrated, Andrea's
parents' views changed. Andrea's mother, once a keen Party member in
Yugoslavia, became very active in the ŽOZ. During a ceramics class, where
Andrea and I met, Andrea told me that her mother de-assimilated from Yugoslavia sometime in the mid-1980s by getting involved in the ŽOZ. Several
years later, when Andrea's mother was forced into early retirement, she took
the initiative to become involved in several different social gatherings, including the Ženska Sekcija. Through her de-assimilation, Andrea's mother transferred her fervent loyalty to communist ideals to ŽOZ politics.

As she fashioned a beautifully elaborate ceramic *menorah*, Andrea
explained that she is interested only in Jewish culture and history, not in
Judaism. She claimed to have inherited these ideas from her parents. She said
that her interest in Jewish culture had grown over time and that although she
would like to learn more about Judaism, she would always consider Judaism
to be information about Jewish cultural history and never the "truth" or the
path to salvation.

*Tamara*

Tamara, a librarian in her late forties, also discovered her Jewish roots when
Croatia transitioned from Yugoslavia. Looking back on her childhood experiences, Tamara has few memories that she is able to trace to a childhood sense
of Jewishness. She recalls an afternoon when her mother was cooking (what
she describes as) "Jewish food," and her parents announced that Adolph
Eichmann had been captured.[1] She remembers her parents being excited
about this incident, which was memorably described to her as a matter of
"justice brought to a terrible man."

During the same time she remembers the slight sarcasm that accompanied
her parents' stories about Jewish religious traditions. For example, although
the purpose of the bar-mitzvah ritual was never fully explained to her or even
mentioned by name, Tamara recalls thinking that backward, uneducated people had bar mitzvahs, and that Eichmann, a high-ranking official in Hitler's
regime, was a common criminal. She explains that anything to do with Judaism, Catholicism, or any other religious expression was completely opaque
to her.

I ran into Tamara frequently at the Friday night services. During our interview, she described herself as a cultural Jew who believes Judaism to be very important to her Jewish identity. She proudly told me that the ŽOZ library is the only one of its kind. She views her work as the ŽOZ's librarian as a way to get involved in the Jewish community and to cultivate her interests in Judaism and Jewish cultural history.

## Zvonko

Zvonko's story is similar to that of Andrea and Tamara insofar as his mother disclosed very little about the Holocaust, embraced *Yugoslavism*, and tried to protect Zvonko from her own past. A pharmacist born after World War II, Zvonko recently became interested in exploring his Jewish background. His mother, who identifies today as a Holocaust survivor, was initially alarmed by Zvonko's decision, but later became interested in her son's search for his newfound identity. Zvonko describes his mother, who raised her two children by herself, as having been vague about her background. Like many Jews who survived World War II, she wanted to insulate her children from her own experiences during the war. She never spoke about her Jewish background, raising Zvonko and his sister practically without any references to her past. Zvonko's mother was a strident supporter of Tito, dressing her children in pioneer outfits as was customary for Tito's birthday celebration. Zvonko remembers running in the relay during these events. As he sees it, his late arrival to Judaism is a consequence of his upbringing. The only time he remembers Jews being mentioned was in connection with his mother's fears about the return of organized anti-Semitism in the 1960s, when she was relieved that Tito did not let the nationalist constituency come to power, and later again in 1991, when Zvonko was already a grown man.

Zvonko's mother saw little to be gained from exposing her children to information about her past once the Yugoslav government collapsed, which she mourned profoundly. She did not hide her Jewish heritage but did not see the need to talk about it or embrace it. Although she is considered Jewish by Jewish law (both her parents were Jewish), she considers herself Croat. Zvonko, on the other hand, rejected that nationality formally (on national census) as well as privately. He became an active participant in ŽOZ services at the time when his mother struggled with Croatia's transition form Yugoslavia. He attended services every Friday night and Saturday morning. Like Tamara, Zvonko continued to nurture his interest in Jewishness through Judaism. It is interesting to note here that Zvonko's sister is not a member of the ŽOZ. Instead, she observes Catholic holidays together with her husband and three young children. Zvonko's own grown children are neither members of the ŽOZ nor particularly interested in their father's or grandmother's backgrounds. Zvonko sees this as the unfortunate result of his children not having grown up in the ŽOZ, due to his own late awareness of his Jewish background.

## *Dubravko*

Dubravko, who works as a security guard at the ŽOZ, showed me a photograph of himself as a longhaired three-year-old that he carried in his wallet. He said that he never understood why his parents had not cut his hair. He had never been able to ask them because they had been killed in the Holocaust when he was only an infant. Dubravko later learned that in the Orthodox tradition a young boy's hair is not cut until he is three years old, information that led him to discover that his parents had been part of a very small minority of Orthodox Jews living in Croatia before 1941. Dubravko, who was adopted by a non-Jewish family, said that he became interested in exploring his Jewish background after the disintegration of Yugoslavia. Despite knowing since the age of ten that his biological parents were Jewish, he did not become interested in his cultural background until Yugoslavia disintegrated. He said that while he had felt a sense of national belonging as a Yugoslav, he had not questioned his cultural identity:

> I always knew that I was somehow different from my parents. I don't mean just the fact that I was adopted. I am not sure why I never acted on my impulses before, but during the euphoria here in Croatia I did not feel I belonged anymore. That's when I decided to pay the Jewish community a visit. Maybe it happened because I lost my homeland. I used to have Yugoslavia. Now I don't have that anymore so I turned to my own people.

Like Mirna, Dubravko relies on symbolic essentialism to make sense of his newfound Jewish identity. Working at the ŽOZ was a way for him to get in touch with a heritage he never knew. He began visiting the ŽOZ at the time when he lost his job in 1993, when Tuđman's nationalism was strong. That same year he was offered a position as a security clerk at the ŽOZ. It was a new position, one that became important after the bombing and reconstruction of the ŽOZ. Outside of his twenty-hour workweek, Dubravko does not visit the ŽOZ or participate in activities there, except for the High Holiday ceremonies. Nevertheless, he insists that his affiliation with the ŽOZ is a "God send," believing that he was "meant to be employed by, and to work for, his own people."

## CULTURAL SIGNIFIERS: NAMES

> My parents suffered so many traumas during [World War II] that they decided that my identity should remain hidden, starting with my name. [After the war] they

called me Jasna, a name that sounds more Croat. But there were problems at school because there was another Jasna. So, they started calling me by my real name, Sarah, to avoid the confusion. I remember getting very upset because I did not even know that was my real name. I screamed: that is not me!

Andrej, a man in his early fifties who liked to meet up with old friends in the *klub*, but who was rarely seen at the *općina* outside of those occasions, agreed to be interviewed in the *klub*, over a strong cup of espresso coffee with whipped cream (a Zagrebian specialty). I knew Andrej primarily through his wife, Ana—a Croat who over the years has become more interested in Jewishness and Judaism than Andrej claims to be. During our interview, I asked Andrej if his father had always had the same last name. This is how he responded:

> No. That is one of those things that is interesting and that will always remain a mystery to me. Father's entire family actually disappeared [in the Holocaust] and those who survived left for Israel even before 1941. The rest of his family was killed: my grandfather, grandmother, and all my father's cousins. I think that his name is a translation of "Friedman," but I am not sure. I never asked him about that because I suppose that it would have been an unpleasant question for him. It might have made him uncomfortable, or maybe he would feel bad about never telling us about it. Perhaps he changed his name, thinking that the Holocaust could happen again. Or perhaps he tried to hide the name in order to protect his descendants from anti-Semitism and other obstacles to leading a fulfilling life. To the present day, I have never asked dad about this, and I am not sure if I am ever going to ask him. He is ninety years old, and thank God he is alive, healthy, and completely clear-headed.

Andrej's narrative resonates with the stories of Andrea, Tamara, and Zvonko. It exhibits the view of Holocaust survivors who aimed to protect their children from their own painful memories. Andrej's narrative also reflects another important criterion in reckoning self-identity—the identification and classification of Jews by non-Jews.

In Croatia, an individual's name reflects ethnic membership and thus social standing in relation to the ethnic majority and the history of the particular group in question. Name recognition was described as one of the most important aspects of identity negotiation. Recall the incident I described in a preceding chapter, where a woman buying a train ticket to Vienna was asked, "Are all you Jews escaping now?" The ticket clerk assumed that the woman was Jewish because of her name.

Having to negotiate name recognition in terms of ethnic membership is even more complicated for intercultural individuals. The tension becomes more pronounced when someone else decides how a person should be identified. Someone with a name like "Cohen" cannot choose to identify as "Croat," or as "Jewish and Croat," or simply as a "world citizen" without having to succumb to the cultural group designation imposed by others.[2] Multiple or inclusive identities are simply contrary to the Croatian norm of single category identity designation.

However, not all Croatian Jews have recognizably "Jewish names." Many German-sounding names are regarded as simply German, thereby allowing Croatian Jews with those names a certain amount of flexibility in terms of identity assertions or alterations.[3] Either way, names are linked to ethnicity, since ethnicity in Croatia is traced along patrilineal lines of descent. This means that someone with a Jewish father and a non-Croat German-sounding family name will be identified as Jewish, regardless of how such a person chooses to identify. ·

This point was brought home to me one day on a visit to a local dry cleaner. In filling out my ticket, the clerk, noting my surname, asked if I was German. When I replied that I was not, the clerk looked confused. So I added that Hofman can be a non-German Jewish as well as a Christian surname. The clerk, undeterred, asked again, "So, are you Jewish?"

In previous centuries, changing one's name or taking on the name of a non-Jewish spouse became a tool for rapid assimilation and social advancement in Croatia. The incentive for name change in the past was mostly driven by economic concerns, since Jews in Croatia, like elsewhere in Europe, were excluded from a number of societies, neighborhoods, and professions. Someone named Fischer who changed his name to Ribar (the same meaning in Croatian as Fisher has in German) thereby increased his chances of full participation in social and political life. Name changes also became important after the war, as the popular name translation from Stern to Zvjezdić implies. The postwar incentive for name change was not economic concerns per se but cultural identity issues. The preoccupation with one's identity characterizes fin de siècle ideologies in Croatia that are driven by an array of global movements that place cultural identity at the center of self-perception.

Dragica is a woman with beautiful gray hair. One of my younger English students, she often brought interesting articles to class and had made enormous efforts to polish her English. After surviving the Holocaust, her father changed his family name from Zuckermann to Cukerić for fear of fascist retaliation. Unlike her father, Dragica is very committed and active in the Jewish community, yet she kept her family name of Cukerić through her last two marriages. In 1994, however, during a period of soul searching and ten years after her father's death, she reversed her father's name change. Her son, who planned to immigrate to Israel in 1999, adopted the reversion to Zuckermann. Dragica's mother, on the other hand, kept the same name Cukerić.

Dragica's story is one of placing cultural identity at the center of one's universe. For Dragica, her last name and her Jewish identity are a celebration.

Dragica's father, on the other hand, did not feel the privilege of embracing his Jewishness as Dragica experiences it today. Having suffered through the Holocaust, the icons that inspire pride in Dragica were, for her father, emblems of fear.

In addition to reflecting ethnic membership, names in Croatia may signify, at least symbolically, political ideologies or other cultural identity markers. For example, in the 1990s, Ivo Goldstein's name became practically synonymous with political critique. Ivo, a Byzantine historian and prominent member of the ŽOZ, is the child of a Croatian and Jewish union in which neither he nor his parents are particularly religious. Like Dragica, he would not be considered Jewish by Jewish religious law. But, unlike Dragica, Ivo claimed in 1997 to identify as a world citizen.

Ivo told me that his colleagues in the history department often consulted him on matters of Jewish history, even though this was never his area of expertise. He had neither written about nor taught Jewish history. The last name of Goldstein led his colleagues to simply assume Ivo's Jewish identity, which, at the time we spoke in 1997–1998, was opaque to him. Since then, and perhaps in spite of it, Ivo has spoken publicly against anti-Semitism in Croatia. His activities have resulted in numerous requests for appearances on various television talk shows as well as public political forms and debates. Like his father, he identifies with the Croatian national cause and supports it, but he did not support the xenophobia of the former HDZ government. Ivo's loyalty to Croatian sovereignty and his ardent public condemnation of anti-Semitism made him—someone who at the time did not self-identify as a Jew—an unofficial spokesperson for the Jewish community.

Ivo's most important critique is directed at the portrayal of the *Ustašas* as patriots and harbingers of the modern Croatian state. For Ivo, the rehabilitation of the image and ideology of the *Ustaša* amounted to a wholesale denial of the atrocities they committed. People like Ivo who write critically about the government are viewed by some as responsible for Croatia's poor international image and are frequently referred to as "Goldsteins," regardless of their cultural background and whether the issue relates to the Jewish community or not. The term rapidly spread in the 1990s, making *Goldstein* synonymous with criticism of the government. Since the time of our interview, Ivo has become a prolific writer on Jewish history in Zagreb and Croatia. During my most recent visit to Zagreb (December 2004), I found Ivo in the ŽOZ library, working on his second book about the history of Jews in Zagreb. Like Tamara, he saw his labor as a way of being involved in the community and a way to leave something behind for his children. In my 2004 conversation with him, I learned that he is more actively involved with ŽOZ politics, serving among other things as the official spokesperson in deliberations about the

*Praška* space. Ivo met with President Mesić and city officials to discuss the *Praška* funding.

## CULTURAL SIGNIFIERS:
## PHYSICAL APPEARANCE

In addition to one's name, physical appearance served as a cultural identity marker in the imagination of both Jews and non-Jews. Michael Montiljo, a former HDZ member and current president of the Croatian Israeli Society, has often been described as "Jewish looking" by both non-Jewish and Jewish Croatians. Based on such views, some members claimed that they would be able to recognize fellow Jews by physical appearance alone. Although contrasts in physical appearance between minorities and the ethnic majority in a given society might be detected if there are vast racialized physical differences, this is not the case for Jews living in Croatia.[4] Ethnic Croats are extremely diversified; they look physically different from border to border. In general, Dalmatians living on the Adriatic Coast are likely to have characteristically darker hair and skin tone than Croats living in the northwestern parts of Croatia. Physical appearances among Croats range from east-central European (i.e., "Slavic features") to Mediterranean and so-called northern European features. Croatian Jews, who are predominately from Ashkenazi backgrounds, are not as easily categorized by their physical characteristics as are Dalmatians, for example.

Ideas about a "Jewish look" are based more on stereotype and a projected Jewish image than on reality. Jakov's story is a good example of this. Jakov, a gentle man in his nineties who is able to trace his Jewish ancestry back five generations, was the first person on either side of his family to marry a non-Jew. Yet Jakov's wife, whom he describes as a pretty brunette, was often perceived as Jewish based on her looks alone: ·

> There are only mixed marriages here [in Croatia]. My wife, for example, is not Jewish even though she looks very Jewish. At least that is what they tell me. But I'll tell you what happened to me when I went to the ŽOZ for the first time and brought her along with me. We were staying with my cousin who lives [in Zagreb]. She and I are the only ones of my family who survived. She was in Auschwitz, and when she came back she went to Israel. But after being in Israel for a couple of years, she returned to Yugoslavia. Anyway, we visited her sometime in 1955. After a couple of days, my cousin asks me, "Do you know what they are saying in the community? What is a pretty Jewish girl (my wife) doing with this Aryan? Where did she find him?" Until this day we laugh about it.

Blond hair and light skin were often perceived as "not Jewish looking" and thus perceived as undesirable. In the ŽOZ, an attractive person was imagined as someone with dark brown eyes, black hair, and olive complexion—representative perhaps of a Mediterranean or Middle Eastern appearance. These stereotypes were reinforced in almost every social event I attended.

Interestingly, Mirna had dyed her hair several shades darker during her cultural transformation. I learned about her change in hair color when she showed me an older picture of herself in which her hair was a much lighter shade. Embarrassed, she failed to comment on it when I asked.[5]

## CONCLUSION

There are several reasons why intercultural Jews regard Jewish identity as an attractive option. Jewish identity is viewed with admiration and awe in part because of the particular history of resistance and against-all-odds survival of Jews in Croatia, together with the xenophobic cultural milieu reintroduced during Tuđman's Croatia. More generally, some individuals with no personal history of Jewish culture find direction through symbolic essentialism, which can often lead to an ardent commitment to the practice of Judaism, as reflected in many of the foregoing interviews with community members.

However, even when newly discovered Jewish identities are negotiated in terms of individually relevant issues, such identities are still strongly influenced by memories of the past. A common sentiment among Holocaust survivors at the *općina* was that they did not want to recall the painful memories associated with the war. The parents of Sarah, Andrea, Tamara, and many others were determined to shield their children from their own Jewish identity in the hopes of somehow protecting them from anti-Semitic or racist experiences.

Alternatively, some parents did not wish to disclose their Jewish background because they felt identification with a Jewish cultural group compromised a prior commitment to Yugoslavian ideals of Brotherhood and Unity. At minimum, membership in the communist collective seemed to render ancestry and cultural background less important, as illustrated by the experience of Andrea's mother. The perception of many Croatian Jews is that solidarity with Yugoslavia was incompatible with identification with Jewish identity. This perception explains why Andrea did not discover her Jewish background until her mother decided to "de-assimilate from communism."

Andrea's story demonstrates the faulty premise in the perception, shared by her mother and many others, of identity as a monolithic feature of the self. Socialized in a non-Jewish, predominately atheist environment, Andrea continued to identify as Yugoslav and Croatian even as she began to explore her newfound Jewish identity. Rather than cultivating a sense of Jewish identity to replace a previous Yugoslav identity, her new identity was, as she put it, a function of "broadening my horizons."

The stories of Tamara, Dubravko, and Zvonko represent the sense of alienation and estrangement that a discovery of one's Jewish identity can produce. Unlike the case of Andrea, their stories emphasize the pain associated with coming to terms with the past. All three narrators wondered what their lives would have been like had they grown up as Jews and participated in Jewish community events as children. They felt a sense of loss about missing those experiences. They also felt loss for their own children, who never participated in ŽOZ events. Worse, their newfound identities have alienated them from their own children. Paradoxically, this unwanted consequence has made Jewish identity even more important for Mirna and Dubravko, who both rely on symbolic essentialism in order to feel connected to their cultural communities and to justify their identities, despite the cost of the resulting estrangement from their families.

In the next chapter, the evolution of the ŽOZ is discussed against the backdrop of the promotion of cultural diversity programs in Croatia and the activities of transnational Jewish support organizations. Accordingly, I examine two wider contexts in which Jewish identity can be conceptualized. In doing so, I argue that the perceived "crisis of Jewish identity" has played an important role in activating support from the Jewish Diaspora. I point out how Croatia's desire to join the European Union is manifested in its promotion of cultural diversity programs and support for the goals of Jewish support organizations. I conclude by arguing that these phenomena are related: both invoke and rely upon a traditionalist view of the Jewish community and Jewish identity.

## NOTES

1. Eichmann was arrested in May 1960 in Argentina and taken to Israel, where he was tried, sentenced, and put to death two years later. The event received much media coverage at the time and has been described by Hannah Arendt (1963).

2. In fact, when I asked interviewees to name five aspects of their self-identity in order of importance, "antifascist" and "world citizen" were the most frequent first or second response. This is what Sarah had to say: "Overall, I have always felt like a world citizen; anything else would be too narrow and limiting to me. I have never been a member of any organization and I don't want to belong to any right now. I guess I belong in a psychological sense to the places that interest me, places where I can learn something new and gain positive experiences."

3. On the other hand, Serbs from mixed marriages living in Croatia who have a recognizable Serbian name are not at liberty to make identity alterations or assertions. Unless they change their name and move to a different place of residence, they continue to be identified by Croatians as Serbs.

4. Such contrasts exist among the dominant group and "minorities." Andrew Buckser (2003) notes that while Danish Jews are convinced that they can recognize fellow Jews from a crowd, they are in fact only observing that these individuals look different from "standard" Danes. The notion of difference is stressed when Jewishness and Danishness are constructed. Ideas community members hold about the physical appearance of in-group and out-group members are in fact more important than the actual appearance of the group.

5. One possible explanation for stereotypes about a "Jewish look" can be found in the redirection of Jews as others, depicted in the past as caricatures of "swarthy looking" Jewish men with large noses, typically hunched over and reading a book. In the anti-Semitic literature Jews were often portrayed as either objects of scorn and repulsion, or as having a special character. According to Garb and Nochlin (1995) Jews were also perceived as intelligent, but "Jewish intelligence" was typically used in an exploitive fashion. Similarly to men, Jewish women were often idealized and portrayed as exotic and excessively sexual in European paintings and texts. This image served as a counterpoint to another image—that of the restrained and proper Christian woman. Ideas that non-Jews hold about Jews are often grounded in historically popular stereotypes that bear little resemblance to reality. The notion of inherited "Jewish noses," a "Jewish character," or of "Jewish traits" became detrimental to European Jewry when it was employed by Nazi propaganda.

## Chapter Six

# Contested Local and Transnational Meanings

I am a Croatian Jew. I consider myself a Jew, and because I was born in Croatia, I also consider myself as a Croat. This is basically because of my culture and education and all my habits put together. I am not a Jew in the sense that I solely identify as a Jew and nothing else. I am not sure if that is possible today anymore. All Jews living in the Diaspora have to confront the eternal problem of duality. Yet some people believe that one cannot be half a Jew, in the sense that a woman cannot be half pregnant; she is either pregnant or not. I used to believe that but I don't anymore. In the end I think that I am a citizen of the world. I feel good everywhere where there are people with whom I can communicate and to whom I don't have to explain or prove who I am.

I met Milan in the *klub* for a cup of tea. We talked about Croatian politics, his job as a sound technician for a local radio station, the ŽOZ, and the meaning of Jewish identity for him. Milan is actively involved in the Jewish community. He writes occasionally for *Ha-kol*, the newspaper of Jewish communities in Croatia. While Milan is considered Jewish by Jewish religious laws, he considers himself Croat as well. As the quotation above indicates, Jewish identity for Milan is riddled with complexities and, more recently, with various shifts in meaning.

Although not the only view, Milan's view is fairly characteristic of Jewish intercultural identity in Croatia. Ethnic designations of Croat and Jew are often viewed as mutually exclusive by Jews abiding by Jewish religious laws and Croats who subscribe to "racially pure" visions of ethnicity. Examined more closely, however, they reveal a range of identity trajectories that are produced by the cultural milieu (local and transnational) in which they are situated.

As we have seen, the stories of ŽOZ members reveal that humanistic Jewish identities are expressed in myriad ways, including through social interaction with fellow Jews. In this chapter, I explore the effects of local and transnational cultural heritage campaigns in shaping the diverse contexts in which Jewish cultural identities are understood. I point out that outside institutions have ignored the desires and wishes of Croatian Jews, who embrace multiple and diverse expressions of identity and community life, not excluding a strong commitment to the humanistic ideals of tolerance, experimentation and contingency. I begin this task by examining how individuals like Milan, who describe themselves as humanistic Jews, negotiate the multiple aspects of their identities.

That discussion is followed by an examination of the incongruous cultural diversity campaigns, sponsored by the Ministry of Culture during and after Croatia's departure from Yugoslavia. The effects of Croatia's departure and the conceptualization of the new nation-state include profound ideological changes with regard to the status of cultural identity in Croatia. I argue that support for cultural diversity in Croatia is connected to the establishment of the new state. The purpose of this is twofold. On the one hand, the endorsement of cultural diversity is designed to appease the European Union, in which Croatia seeks membership. On the other hand, it continues to validate cultural differences between Croats and non-Croats and to thereby reinforce idealized or xenophobic perceptions of Jews, as distinct from other Croatian citizens.

The last section of this chapter examines the effects of transnational heritage campaigns on Jewish community life in Croatia. As we have seen in previous chapters, the focus of transnational Jewish support organizations has shifted in response to the characterization of Jewish identity in east-central Europe and elsewhere as in *crisis*. Therefore, the cultivation of religiosity and the promotion of a separatist Jewish identity have been emphasized in an attempt to escape this so-called crisis. I once again challenge the premise that Jewish identity is in crisis by arguing that the crisis theory rests on a notion of Jewish identity based on essentialist or traditionalist principles that are contrary to the self-images of Croatian Jews themselves.

## HOW CROATIAN JEWS DEFINE THEMSELVES: HUMANISTIC EXPRESSIONS OF JEWISH IDENTITY

The majority of Croatian Jews are humanistic Jews who express their identity in myriad ways. Cultural heritage symbols, such as religious artifacts, food, festivals, and other social activities, are important for expressing cultural identity. In the ŽOZ, the importance of these symbols is reflected in the popularization of Star of David pendants, *menorahs*, and other *Judaica* (Jewish religious artifacts) that is either worn or exhibited at home. When I asked about the particular meanings associated with these material expressions of Jewish cultural heritage, Ljerka told me the following:

> I would like to have my children brought up in a Jewish spirit. So, I decorate my house with paintings of Jewish artists, Shabbat candles, books related to Judaism, and Jewish dance and music CDs. By exposing them to these things and to the community I can only hope that they will become Jews. I want my kids to be familiar with these things from an early age because I believe that that is the only way that they can learn.

Material objects such as the ones described function as articulations of Jewish identity and, as Ljerka notes, learning tools. I observed further evidence of the emergence of heritage symbols in Croatia in the 1990s by the popularization of Jewish cookbooks written by Croatian Jews and the proliferation of various books, newspapers, lectures, and radio programs addressing Jewish themes. In addition to these, as discussed in previous chapters, ŽOZ members can join a Jewish folkloric dance group, ceramics class, and, with a little luck, participate in the *Makabiada* (Jewish Olympic Games). They can choose to study Hebrew, Jewish music, Jewish history, or Torah in Jewish community centers. Almost all the ŽOZ members regard these pursuits (including Torah reading) as leisure social activities and are not for the sake of practicing religiosity or living a "traditional" Jewish life according to Jewish law. Instead, they are seen as an expression of cultural heritage or interest in Jewish cultural history. Since many of these activities are organized by the *općina*, these vehicles of identity enactment require social interaction among group members.

It is in this sense that the ŽOZ functions as the hub of social activities for people of all ages. Friendships made in childhood continue into old age. Community members who met in the ŽOZ kindergarten expressed that they have nurtured bonds established in early childhood throughout their lives. Summer camps such as Pirovac, where Jewish youths from Yugoslavia once met and Croatian Jews continue to meet, contribute to the long-lasting friendships and humanistic expressions of Jewish identity. This is a fairly typical example from Jasenka, a retired ŽOZ member, who explained how she likes to spend her time when visiting the center:

> I used to be a member of the cultural society. I collaborated with Lea's mom. I have to admit that for a few years now since I have gotten a little bit older I am not so active anymore, but I very often attend the classes here and the concerts. There are very interesting things here and many of my girlfriends who I have known for over

half a century come here. Just tonight, I will go to see a documentary they are show-
ing downstairs. We will probably have tea afterwards and catch up. I am very committed, in that manner, emotionally and by being present, to the community.

This sentiment is echoed among members of the younger generation as well,
as exemplified by the comments of Goran:

Mom brought me to the community, even though she is not Jewish, when I was very
little. I attended preschool here. I also went to Sunday school and was sent went to
Pirovac. The entire Jewish youth from Yugoslavia was there. I have beautiful memories of that time and all my closest friends are from the community.

I asked Goran, How often do you visit the community today?

Well kind of, I do not know—we usually meet in the center of the city and then go
to the community. Sometimes I come to the community by myself, drink coffee, you
always find somebody you know and can talk to. Sometimes I come on Mondays to
watch the girls dance upstairs or I go to the fitness center in the basement here. I
like to punch the bag for a little while, punch out my negative energy. Then there
are the Thursday nights when we all meet on the second floor [in the *klub*] around 8
pm. Come to think of it, I am here pretty often.

Jewish community centers in Croatia experienced a revival during the late
1980s and early 1990s as Jewish educators were brought in from abroad to
teach Hebrew, Jewish culture, and history. A cultural society that hosted lectures and events like Jewish music and exhibits of Jewish Croatian artists was
formed during that time, now referred to as "Jewish community revival."
While the society published a monthly paper covering events pertinent to the
Jewish world, the events themselves did more than educate the public about
Jewish life. For Croatian Jews, partaking in activities hosted by the cultural
society was seen as an important way of "being Jewish" or "getting in touch
with one's roots." Participation in community events was considered central
to the process of making Jewish identity meaningful in Croatia. It was
thought by Sonja that Croatian Jews made sense of their world and made
choices about their identities only through participation in various social
groups. Intercultural community members did so without necessarily dismissing other parts of their heritage. As Sonja, an active environmentalist,
explained one day to me when we hiked in *Sljeme*, the mountain range that
surrounds Zagreb,

I think that it [Jewish cultural identity] is strong and dual for us. This is a common
phenomenon for [intercultural] Jews, not something special for Zagreb. I think that
the Jews who live in the Diaspora have always had a dual sense of belonging. Only
the Israelis do not have this problem. That is, if it is considered a problem at all.

Jews around the world are fitted more or less into the environment in which they live. So, I think that it is inevitable that we all have a dual identity regardless of whether we married a Catholic or not. I felt these multiple alliances during Yugoslavia and I still feel them today. I was a big Yugoslavian patriot, and yet at the same time I felt very strongly that I belonged to the Jewish people.

Like many Croatian Jews, Sonja refers to Croats as Catholics. This is because Catholics in Croatia are an unmarked, or normative, cultural group, like WASPs in the United States. Zoran is a political science student who is actively involved in Motek, a publication that details the lives of ŽOZ youth. Here is his more youthful take on intercultural identity:

I am a Croatian Jew because I am from Croatia. As much as I love my Jewish origins, I love my Croatian origins as well. The Jewish side of my family is actually not from Croatia but from Riga [former Soviet Union]. They ended up in Croatia by chance. The part of my family that settled in Croatia survived the Holocaust. The rest, except for the ones who are in America, were killed.

Like Milan, Zoran stressed that feeling Croat, Croatian, and Jewish did not present a conflict for him. He was concerned with the rise of xenophobia in Croatia and the views of those on the right, but stressed that people with those views did not inhabit his world.

On the whole, community members seemed to be more concerned with day-to-day social affairs and Croatian politics than with high exogamy rates or Jewish religious laws. Nevertheless, I saw Zoran and many other people I have talked to attending the monthly Family Sabbath gathering. Although the weekly Sabbath service has never attracted large crowds in Croatian communities, a small but stable group attends Friday night services, discussion groups on Saturday morning, and the more popular monthly Family Sabbath. Most of the Family Sabbath crowd does not attend the services, but waits in the *klub* on the second floor until the service goers join them, thus making the character of these gatherings primarily social. When I asked Zoran how he understood the role of religiosity in the continuation of Jewish community life in Zagreb, I was given the following explanation:

I don't think our community will die because we are intermarrying or not praying on Friday night. In the end a community dies when people stop visiting the community. It is clear that the people here are coming to the *općina* for something. The *općina* does not exist by itself. If one takes Jewish identity to mean religion then probably our community is in trouble. However, if you take it mean something else then . . . are you not writing about this? What is your take on it? Whenever people first showed up [in the ŽOZ] it was as a result of some Jewish identity. They felt something. Whether it is some impulse or interest in the sense that they have nowhere to go, that is difficult to say. But [the community] exists and I think it will continue to exist.

When asked directly, community members associated religiosity with doctrine, nationalism, and noncosmopolitanism. Indeed, many people I spoke with did not regard religious practice as an important part of their Jewish identity. Friday night services were practically empty while social events organized by the cultural society were well attended. Yet Judaism was seen as important cultural knowledge. Jadranka, who has been raised in the ŽOZ community and whose young child is in the ŽOZ kindergarten, remarked,

I believe that Judaism gives us the freedom and the opportunity to choose how to express ourselves as Jews. I have chosen the way I wish to be Jewish. I have met people who have chosen to keep kosher. A kosher couple visited me recently. I did not insult or asked them why they kept kosher. I don't keep kosher but I always make sure I have paper plates, plastic knives and forks at home in case they visit.

Jadranka's visitors were from abroad. In fact, for the few observant Jews, keeping kosher is quite a challenge. One woman I met traveled to Hungary (on a Saturday, the Orthodox Jewish day of rest) to purchase kosher foods. She explained that Saturday was the only day she could travel to Hungary because she works during the week. Traveling on the Shabbat did not appear to be a compromise for her. Since she did not keep kosher, consuming kosher foods was more an expression of her Jewish identity than observing Jewish religious laws. On closer inspection, I learned that only a handful of people in the community grew up with kosher food and a firmly observant Jewish religious life—namely, those born prior to World War II who still remembered those experiences. More prevalent were members who remembered very little, if anything, about their religious education. Dunja, one of my English language students who supplied me with vivid details about her Jewish life, said,

Nothing else was there [in terms of religious education], just Yom Kippur. Dad would fast because it was related to all of the people that had died. I remember the candlesticks burning and dad fasting. He would work all day long, which was very difficult for him, because he was a big, fat man. Fasting probably meant a lot of suffering to him. I remember mom making thick chicken soup to end the fasting and his suffering. That was our experience of kosher.

Since she did not grow up in the Jewish culture, I asked Dunja how she understood the change in her identity. She explained that she got in touch with her Jewish heritage as a teenager when visiting the *općina* for the first time:

I did not know what being a "Jew" meant. I remember when I was very little, I went home and asked my mom what it was, but I do not remember the answer I received. I don't know what her explanation of it was. Looking back, I think that they were stupid for pushing their heads in the sand. During [my quest] to find out what a Jew is, my friend brought me here [to the ŽOZ]. I liked coming there for completely non-Jewish reasons. From the first time I went to the community I felt accepted. I liked that and continued coming once a week. The community was something that completely enriched my life. I felt that wherever I would go I would have friends. To me it is an absolutely beautiful memory, especially because of a pan-Yugoslavian Judaism that dominated. You had a feeling that you were not alone, that there were many people like you. It was an incredible opportunity for us kids to bond. I just needed to make a phone call [to a Jewish community center in Yugoslavia] and there was always somebody there for you to put you up for the night, have coffee with you, or help you with something you needed. It was a very nice feeling [of community] that not too many people get to experience. I had so many friends, I never really thought about them specifically as being Jewish. We got along well, so we obviously had something in common. You know I never asked my mother about dad's fasting.

Even though Dunja's view puts her in the minority of her fellow observant ŽOZ members, she shares with nonobservant Jews a sense of freedom and opportunity to modify her identity as she wishes.

For intercultural Jews, the freedom and opportunity to choose one's identity did not always come without a price. This is what Tanja (another of my language group students) had to say:

I think that there is very little opportunity for Jewish marriages [in Croatia]. Maybe one out of thirty marriages is between two natural-born Jews. Most others in our community are mixed marriages. There are many cases in which the wives are devoted [to the cultural heritage of their Jewish husbands]. I am not sure if you know doctor S and his wife B? She is so dear. She does all of that [being involved in Jewish cultural events] with him. She completely sides with him. Do you know our friend Vera D? Her son is in Venezuela. His wife is *very* Jewish. I think that she even converted to Judaism. It's a funny thing because he is not a particularly religious man. Next to him, she would not be able to be any different because he is a true Jew . . . but not in the religious sense of course. Now I have no such luck. My nephew, who got married to a Catholic woman, had his children baptized. The children got their first Communion, second Communion, their Confirmation, and I do not know what all else but it is all tied to her side of the family. The outcome of that union is very sad to me. My nephew and his wife come to the ŽOZ concerts and other events. But when there is an event that is specifically Jewish, they do not go. It is clear that she is the boss in their marriage.

The same sentiment of individual opportunity and the responsibility to pass on one's cultural heritage to one's child through material culture was echoed by Sonja (who is intermarried) when I asked her if it is important to her that her sons marry a Jewish woman. When I asked her how she felt about mixed marriages, and if she cared that her future daughters-in-law would be Croats or Serbs, she replied,

> Well I have to say that it is important to me. I mean, that is not a nice thing to say, but frankly I have to say if I was really sincere that it is important to me. First of all I have boys, so everything stops with them if they do not have a wife who is Jewish because it's women who usually bring culture to the family. But, let's say, one of them married a girl that grew up the way that I did or the way that the two of them did, just in a completely different country. I think that there would be a problem. I think that their children would no longer have a sense of belonging anywhere. But if she grew up in Croatia and was open to our ways, I would be very satisfied. I think that if there is a Jew somewhere in the family the person can decide if he is a Jew or not. I have met people in America who are natural-born Jews but don't identify as Jews. So, you see, everything is possible.

The foregoing quotations emphasize predominantly humanistic expressions of Jewish identity. The people I interviewed believed that Judaism or Jewish cultural heritage gave them the "freedom and opportunity to choose" how to express identity, including the option of abandoning cultural distinctiveness and religious observance. A remarkably frequent observation was that they identified as "world citizens" or, as Milan put it, as "humanistic Jews." Study participants stressed the fact that they perceived self-identification as a matter of choice, and that their choice was most frequently that of a world citizen.

## HOW JEWISH OUTSIDERS DEFINE CROATIAN JEWISH IDENTITY: THE INCONGRUITY OF CULTURAL DIVERSITY IN CROATIA

One day at the ŽOZ I met Sonja, the former representative of the Council of National Minorities in Croatia. Sonja served on the council as the representative of the Jewish community during the council's existence from 1998 to 2003. She explained that the council had a strong influence on the formation of the constitutional laws that affect minorities in postcommunist Croatia. From our conversation, it became clear that constitutional legislation (first established as the *Constitutional Law of Human Rights and National Minorities*, and later as the *Constitutional Law of National Minorities*), drafted in 1992, had not been implemented until 2001. The laws were prerequisites to Croatia's eligibility for membership in the European Union. But, as Sonja pointed out, such laws are also very important for the national minorities living in Croatia:

[The laws] opened up many human rights issues in Croatia. It was awfully important that we were in very close collaboration with the outside world such as the Venice commission. The Venice commission is a commission of the lawyers of the Council of Europe that engage in democracy through law. It is an exceptional group of people who monitor transitional countries like this one in terms of human rights issues. Even though we did not take part in drafting legislation, we made many suggestions that are incorporated into law today. Although a lot more work needs to be done, the council exposed the issues minority groups had been struggling with in Croatia and continues to do so till the present.

The official goal of the 1990s cultural diversity campaigns in Croatia was to increase the visibility of minorities. However, those campaigns' representation of minorities was constructed to mark insiders and outsiders, and to thereby assert political and ideological power. Examples of support for such goals include legislation that supported minority-based community centers, state subsidies for native language courses, and support for the religious practices of a number of minority groups. According to Milena Klajner (1997), laws passed in 1996 reflect "the highest standards of rights of ethnic minorities," and are therefore "paving the way towards acceptance into various European associations." Klajner cautions that the removal of Article 24, since 1945, had made anti-Semitic and racist acts punishable by law.

The effects of minority regulations for Croatian Jews are double-edged. While the development has resulted in subsidies and support for the Jewish community, it has also fueled anti-Jewish xenophobia by reinforcing an image of Jews as outsiders. The diversity campaigns are only one example of how the imagined cultural differences between ethnic Croats and nonethnic Croats have become more pronounced. With the emergence of the Croatian Roman Catholic revival and exclusionist nationalism came the construction of otherness. A foreigner, someone who did not *rightfully* belong, became a potential national threat. The threat was mostly symbolic, signaling the preoccupation of right wing Croats with their own ethnicity, but views such as these were prominent during the transitional period of the early 1990s.

Ethnic Serbs living in Croatia felt the consequences of exclusionist nationalism most harshly. This is what Mira, an intercultural Serb, had to say about having to apply for citizenship documents during Croatia's transition in 1991:

We all had to apply for citizenship papers. The forms came in the mail. They asked you to write down which ethnic group you belonged to. Until that time, I had been declared as a Yugoslav. My mom and dad were responsible for that decision. But in 1991, as an adult woman, I declared myself as a Jew. I had several options. Since all my options were minority [designations], I had to go to the Ministry of the Interior in order to get my papers. Those who did not declare themselves as a Croat had to go to the ministry or the police. Croats just mailed in their application They were not questioned about who they were. At the ministry, they asked questions about my parents. Specifically, they asked a lot of questions about my dad, who lives in Serbia and is divorced from my mom. I learned that I was at one point listed as "belonging to Serbia" because I was born there and perhaps also because of my father. They looked at my passport, asked who financed my traveling "abroad," which was to Yugoslavia [the Serb republic], and asked what my dad does for a living in Belgrade and so on and so forth. I felt very uncomfortable. They kept focusing on the Serb part, never the Jewish part, even though that's how I declared myself. It was as if they did not believe me, as if I had imagined my background. I had to pay four times as much for the paperwork than people who declared themselves as Croats, and I had to make several trips to the ministry. I heard from my Serbian friends that they had troubles too.

The gradual erosion of Tito's Yugoslavia led to a reformulation of the meaning of collective identity and nation building. Those on the far right began articulating Jewish identity as something that was merely imagined. After all, many believed that World War II had destroyed the entire Jewish population. In an April 1998 interview on Radio 101, the host interviewer asked Ognjen Kraus president of the ŽOZ, why he thought Jews as a minority group in Croatia were receiving so much press. Kraus told me that the inter-viewer put the question to him as follows:

> How many Jews are there in Croatia? The reason I am asking this is because there are not enough Jews in Croatia to have a political voice or form a threat or evoke some sort of imagined hatred. In fact, I have never even heard of a radio program on other so-called ethnic minorities.

One popular notion during the transition was that Croatian Jews were somehow dishonest about their cultural background and that Jews were enjoying political clout as a result of the so-called Jewish lobby. The sheer presence of ethnic minorities (imagined or not) was contrary to the Yugoslav ideal of unity. During Croatia's nation-state building program, ethnic minor-ity cultures were viewed as unfaithful to the ideals of Croatian nationhood, and therefore unfaithful to Croatia's international image. Depicted as disloyal to the state, individual Jews and the Jewish community became the targets of a variety of stereotypes, including the view that Croatian Jews are *Yugonos-talgics*, Serb-lovers or opportunists, profiting from the aid of the so-called international Jewish lobby. We have already seen in previous chapters how the ŽOZ became the target of a hate-crime bombing in 1991. Another exam-ple of this is the 1998 attack on historian Ivo Goldstein for misrepresenting Croatian history. Goldstein, an intercultural Jew born and raised in Croatia, whose mother and wife are Croats, was asked in an interview, "Why should non-Croatians teach Croatians about *their* history?"

While skepticism about the legitimacy of a Jewish identity remained, acknowledging the existence of Croatian Jews—indeed, *celebrating* it—proved more useful than questioning its legitimacy. This has been played out most visibly in Croatia's bid to join the European Union. In order to construct a new vision of the state, the old Yugoslav model of Brotherhood and Unity needed to be replaced by a contemporary vision of cultural diversity celebration. The promotion of the Jewish *religious* community, along with the celebration of a separate Roman Catholic Croat identity, fit neatly with the goals of this project.

In order to underscore the nation's separateness, Croatia assumed an identity that continues to be inseparable from the political discourse of Tuđman's regime. In a 1998 self-congratulatory address to the nation, Tuđman said that bringing Croatia back to Europe meant a radical separation from the East:

> This achievement [Croatia's secession from Yugoslavia], the realization of a dream cherished by the Croatian people for nine centuries, actually for a millennium, is the work of the Program of the Croatian Democratic Union, of its leadership and of all its members, and of the majority of the Croatian people.

The importance of Croatia's membership in the European Union continues to be viewed as crucial to the betterment of the Croatian economy. More importantly, however, membership links the country's cultural and geopolitical transformations. Membership in the European Union would facilitate economic and political relations between Croatia and European Union countries. It would also provide Croatia with political security and, most importantly, situate Croatia in a *civilized* Europe where, as some like to believe, she has always belonged.

The European Union imposed tough political and economic prerequisites for membership. Predictably, Croatia responded by adopting numerous human rights declarations and legal provisions designed to abolish racial discrimination. However, as we saw from Sonja's account, these were not implemented until 2001. Most of the documents pertaining to constitutional and legal rights for ethnic minorities function to maintain de jure nondiscrimination, equality, and freedom of expression. Yet, what Christopher Cviic (1995) pointedly calls Croatia's "democratic deficits" are among the main reasons why Croatia was not ready to apply for membership to the European Union until February 2003. Cviic's list of the most important reasons for this deficit includes human rights violations, manipulation of the state-controlled news media, prevention of genuine freedom of speech through the printed media, the anti-democratic practices of the HDZ government and its aftermath, and the state's manipulation of the judiciary.

In the mid-1990s, the right grew louder (although not larger), and xenophobia began to be seen as a real threat to Jews. This fear was reinforced by the Croatian government's attempt to repress memories associated with the notorious *Ustašas*. This was accomplished by downplaying the atrocities that the *Ustašas* committed during World War II against the Serbs, Roma, communists, noncompliant Croats, and Jews. The *Ustašas* themselves were constructed as the victims of Tito's National Liberation Army revolt. Tributes to the victims of World War II, such as the Victims of Fascism Square, were erased. These changes were aimed to symbolically oppose Brotherhood and Unity and to imagine the new geopolitical position of Croatia.

An important response to the hegemonic new social order was the development of solidarity among Croatian minorities. Many continue to gather and mark events such as Anti-Fascism Day and Holocaust Memorial Day. For example, demonstrations were organized to oppose the name change of the Victims of Fascism Square. As one demonstrator explained, "Changing the name of the square [back to its original name] is an opportunity for Croatia to begin the process of *de-Ustashization.*"

Another symbolic area of contention has been the number of victims who perished in Jasenovac, a Croatian concentration camp established during the *Ustaša* regime. Some have claimed that the number of lives lost in Jasenovac is as low as forty thousand, while others estimate the death toll around seven hundred thousand. In 1997, Tuđman proposed erecting a memorial for victims and murderers at the same site. The proposal was met with outrage and caused large numbers of people to gather in protest on Holocaust Memorial Day in April 1998. Among those who protested were individuals who identified as antifascist and former communists. Speakers called for justice, the restoration of Jasenovac as a memorial and respect for the memory of the victims. They warned that the number of victims should be neither belittled nor buried along with the remains of their executioners.

As a result of the protests, Croatian citizens began criticizing Tuđman's politics. The *Feral Tribune*, a weekly newspaper that was nearly shut down by the government in 1999, has made its reputation largely by ridiculing Croatian national politics. Its political satire served as a powerful opposition to right-wing politics and proposals, like Tuđman's Jasenovac memorial. In response to threats to close down newspapers such as the *Feral Tribune* and the fiercely independent Radio 101, Croatians asserted their right to freedom of speech.

At the same time, the Ministry of Culture made several attempts to educate Croatians about Jewish culture. Programs about Jewish culture aired on local television and radio stations. National television broadcast Jewish folkloric dance and music at the Minorities Celebration festival. Sitting in the audience of the festival in 1998, I overheard whispered conversations questioning why Jews were considered a minority. Jewish religious practices, often misunderstood and regarded as curious by non-Jewish Croatians, received an abundance of media attention in the 1990s. Local journalists interviewed the chief rabbi of Croatia several times since his inauguration in 1998. The topics of these interviews ranged from Jewish religious practices to the future of the Jewish community in Croatia. Television programs about Jewish religious laws and practices as well as foreign documentaries, which depicted the lives of ultra-Orthodox Jews, were aired. The Ministry of Culture also provided funds for Jewish education centered on Jewish religious and cultural themes and invited the rabbi to the Croatian parliament on several occasions.

As Croatia's national euphoria began to fade, the country's socioeconomic problems were exposed. This has made inclusion in the European Union and the global marketplace highly desirable. Membership in the European Union has been defined as one of the most important goals for Croatia's economic and political future. In an attempt to reach this goal and to appear more Western, Croatia has presented herself as a nation that promotes cultural diversity. The imagined cultural divisions described earlier have ultimately been designed to create political divides between "the old system" and the "new democracy," which aligns Croatia closer to a civilized Europe.

## HOW JEWISH OUTSIDERS DEFINE CROATIAN JEWISH IDENTITY: THE GLOBAL JEWISH VILLAGE

Nothing similar to our community has ever existed here. Sure there were [cultural] communities, there still are, but there was no such connection between people. That connection goes from way back because our parents knew each other in Yugoslavia. So, we don't have just our own memories but the memories of our parents. That is what gives us this incredible intertwining feeling. Considering that Jews today have even more connections with people in countries outside of Croatia, one can say that the entire Jewish world is actually a village. That is a very pleasant feeling because one never feels lost. It is kind of a feeling of security. I can always count on calling someone from the Jewish community wherever I am in the world.

Mima, who used to belong to the Communist Party during Yugoslavia, talked about the profound meaning the Jewish community has for her in terms of long-lasting friendships and Jewish cultural opportunities for her two kids. We talked about the power of friendship and family networks that for her are deeply rooted in the community. She told me how she grew up in the ŽOZ during Yugoslavia. She met her husband in the community and both her children are involved in Jewish community life. Mima and her husband are one of the rare couples in the community who are not intercultural Jews.

Mima explained to me that the ŽOZ and the wider Yugoslav Jewish community have always supplied her with a support-network. Today, her network has international proportions.

Mima points out that since the disintegration of Yugoslavia and the emergence of the Croatian nation-state, transnational linkages have gained prominence. This has enabled Jews around the world to communicate with one another. As she sees it, Croatian Jews have more connections with Jews living in countries outside of Croatia and the former Yugoslavia than ever before.

As the ideal of Brotherhood and Unity began to disintegrate after Tito's death in 1980, political reforms swept through much of east-central Europe. Belief in the importance of Jewish education grew and Jewish educators in Croatia were brought in from abroad sometime in the mid-1980s. The educators focused primarily on Jewish collective history, holidays, and Hebrew language instruction. Social conditions pointed to an imminent collapse of Yugoslavia and the social order but there was no concept of what would come after the collapse. The atmosphere has been described as apocalyptic. Religious revival movements such as the miracle of *Medjugorje* (the appearance of the Virgin Mary on the Croatian/Bosnian border) and a number of western as well as eastern religious movements were on the rise. For the first time, Mormons, Hare Krishna worshipers, and other marginal groups found a following in Croatia. At the same time, an emphasis on Roman Catholic Croatian identity arose that was strongly connected to Croatian nationalism. Dormant Croatian Catholic heroes, especially those who had been nationalist in orientation during the *Ustaša* regime, were revived and later canonized by the pope in Rome. Campaigns to purify the Croatian language occurred during the early stages of the transition. Croatian words that had not been used for nearly a century were invigorated. *Ustaša* symbolism reemerged and the Right acquired a voice that had been silenced under communism. Everything pointed towards the revitalization of old dormant symbols and neoconservative family values. Jewish community revival was conceived under these social conditions, coinciding with Croatia's rapidly transforming political climate in the 1990s.

For Croatian Jews such as Mima, the collapse of Yugoslavia combined with acculturation to Yugoslav ideals meant that different strategies had to be sought for sustaining social equality and nondiscrimination. This meant having to negotiate a de facto outsider status. In fact, an even greater involvement in Jewish communal life provided a reasonable alternative to the changing meaning of Croatian national identity for many Jews during the transition. A renewed connection with the Jewish community served the function of ideologically forestalling social isolation from Croatian society. Membership in the Jewish community had other advantages as well. For example, during the war in Croatia (1991–1995) community members were able to send their children to stay with families in the United States, Canada, and Israel. These temporary immigrations were sponsored by Jewish communities abroad.

I asked interviewees and several other ŽOZ members whether they had maintained contact with the Jews they had met abroad. Many said they had little contact with Israelis including their relatives. Even fewer Jews maintained contacts with family members or people they had met in the United States and Canada. Those who had been sent to the United States as teenagers during the war and those who had immigrated (temporary or otherwise) to Israel expressed feeling culturally alienated from the host societies in which they had lived. The stress of the war and being separated from friends and family may have contributed to this. But many young people from the community told stories about returning back to Croatia after having lived in Israel for some time (this was well before the intensification of the Palestinian-Israeli conflict). The only exceptions were the few individuals who had departed for Israel in order to maintain a religious life. Almost everyone else felt alienated and described being treated, together with former Soviet Union (FSU) Jews, as illegitimate. Dragan, who came back in less than a year from Israel, said, "The Israelis questioned whether we were real or imaginary Jews. They always acted suspicious when we said that we are from Croatia. It was the same for them as saying that we are from Russia." Dragan's account places Mima's observations into perspective. Perhaps the most contact ŽOZ members have with other Jewish institutions is through the influence of the transnational organizations.

## TRANSNATIONAL JEWISH ORGANIZATIONS

In the early to mid-1990s, activities sponsored by the transnational organizations were increasingly concerned with Jewish spiritual education. Such organizations perceived the task before them as rescuing Jews from the evils of communism and rehabilitating them into Jews for whom religious concerns would be paramount. Organizations interested in boosting Jewish religious education saw east-central Europe in the late 1980s as an untapped opportunity for *aliyah* (immigration) to Israel. Sometime in the mid-1990s, the "opportunity" for conversion and endogamy was extended. Neoconservative in orientation, the ideas of the sponsors of these organizations related directly to the perception that Jews are on the brink of extinction. The ultra-Orthodox Lubavitich, for example, advanced its agenda by supplying materials for Jewish educational purposes throughout Eastern Europe. Anita Weiner (2003) writes that in many places in Eastern Europe, and in particular the FSU, only the ultra-Orthodox responded actively to Jewish educational opportunities. It is worth noting that missionary work of the sort practiced by the ultra-Orthodox is not common to other (more traditional) branches of Judaism. It is, however, consistent with the belief among ultra-Orthodox Jews that the maintenance of Jewish religiosity is one of the most pressing social concerns facing contemporary Jewish communities around the world.

Jewish organizations active in the FSU reported rehabilitation activities since the earliest days of *Glasnost* and *Perestroika*, when Jewish identity was declared an endangered species in Eastern Europe. In 1994 Edgar Bronfman, president of the World Jewish Congress (WJC), warned that the Jewish community was on the verge of collapse: "For a couple of generations our Jewishness has been expressed by our devotion to the State of Israel and our checks to the United Jewish Agency (UJA). But now that Israel is moving towards peace with its neighbors, it will not command the same attention" (Goldberg, 1994). Of course, the conflict between Israel, the Palestinians, and the rest of the Muslim world has not been resolved. Yet Bronfman continues to maintain that the great challenge facing world Jewry in the future is to find a way to provide the younger generation with a sense of spiritual mission. Regeneration strategies stressed Jewish education by establishing full-time Orthodox rabbis in community centers such as the ŽOZ.

Among the most important goals of organizations such as the WJC and the UJA is to help Jews throughout east-central Europe to reconnect with their Jewish cultural heritage.[1] Since 1988, organizations such as the American Jewish Joint Distribution Committee (JDC) have supported Jewish kindergartens and day schools, as well as Hebrew and Jewish history courses in Croatia and other east-central European countries. The JDC and the WJC have also played important political roles in securing the rights of Jewish communities in east-central Europe. In Croatia, these organizations stressed the reestablishment of diplomatic ties with Israel and have launched several campaigns involving European governments in restitution proceedings for Holocaust victims.[2]

Religious Jewish education was and continues to be sponsored primarily by the ultra-Orthodox in Croatia as in many other countries in east-central Europe. In contrast, a Jewish school established in Zagreb in 2003 (first to twelfth grade) was sponsored in part by the Croatian government and American Orthodox constituencies, which have different educational objectives than the JDC and the WJC. In its opening year, the Jewish school in Zagreb had twelve children enrolled in the first grade, nine of whom (or 75 percent) were either intercultural Jews or Croats, including the grandchild of Stjepan Mesić, the Croatian president. I spoke to one of three young women who teach in the school. The rabbi recruited the women (ŽOZ members and intercultural Jews) after they graduated from high school in 1999. The woman I spoke with (who asked that her name be withheld) described the following experience to me:

> We were sent to Israel because the rabbi wanted people who could teach Hebrew and Judaism to kids in Zagreb. Since my experience working at different summer camps, I knew that some day I would like to work with children. So when the news came that the three of us received a scholarship for a teaching academy in Israel I was thrilled. However, in Israel we had somewhat of a shock. We did not know what it meant to be dressed in skirts, long sleeves all the time or to be at a religious place, and to be taught by rabbis. The program we attended lasted for two years. We studied Judaism and Hebrew and had some general pedagogy classes. We did our student training at the Maimonides school, a very religious elementary school. The rabbi told us when we came back from Israel that the purpose of our education was working in the new school. He also explained that elementary school pedagogy alone was not enough for the school. There had to be some kind of a Jewish education present. How else were we going to teach at the school?

Emphasizing the religious components of Jewish identity, Orthodox organizations began rehabilitating Jewish community centers throughout Croatia and the former Yugoslavia by financing full-time rabbis, rebuilding several synagogues (the most noteworthy in Dubrovnik, a community of less than fifty Jews) and stressing Jewish religious education. The chief rabbi of Croatia (the rabbi of the ŽOZ) found sponsors among Orthodox communities outside the country to finance young Croatian Jews' religious education abroad. Changes have been implemented in the community centers themselves. Regardless of the number of members at a given community or the level of participation in community events, the rabbi engaged in the koshering of community centers throughout Croatia. He has implemented various Jewish laws in the centers and campaigned for group conversion to counteract high exogamy rates. He has also provided opportunities for those interested in studying and practicing Orthodox Judaism and making *aliyah* to Israel. In many ways, the rabbi has revolutionized the social organization of Jewish communities in Croatia. For the first time in sixty years, Croatian Jews can choose to get married in a Jewish Orthodox ceremony and have a local rabbi perform rites of passage (e.g., circumcision, bar mitzvah, marriage, and burial ceremonies) and important Jewish holidays. However, as a result of the rabbi's views, ŽOZ members are not exposed to the wide variety of approaches to Judaism. For example, bat mitzvah, the coming of age ceremony for young women installed by non-Orthodox Judaism is not recognized and therefore not tolerated in the ŽOZ. Neither are personalized burial rites that are more inclusive and representative of the intercultural reality of the ŽOZ. One of the main sources of tension between the community rabbi and the members has been a lack of a common cultural base. In previous chapters we saw that although ŽOZ members are not particularly interested in Orthodox Judaism, they regard the presence of a rabbi as important to their community. They are, however, divided over what type of a person the rabbi should be.

## CONCLUSION

Croatia's desire to disassociate itself with communism and to be included among Europe's "chosen nations," is well served by promoting nonthreatening minorities such as Croatian Jews. The promotion of Croatian Jews not only obscures Croatia's role in the Holocaust—an issue that received critical attention from the international media and from human rights organizations—but emphasizes Jews as "others." The cultural diversity programs sponsored by the Croatian Ministry of Culture are premised on the view that Jews must be submerged in tradition and religion. These cultural diversity programs "advancing" Jewish religious culture do not exist for the promotion of a genuinely inclusive multicultural society. Instead, these programs have particular agendas that seek to promote Croatian Jews as exotic, religious, and different from ethnic Croatians.

As we have seen, although their motivations differ, Croatia's cultural diversity programs share with the international Jewish support organizations the tendency to promote identity maintenance by reifying differences between cultural groups and exaggerating the importance of religious consciousness. Although the objectives of Croatian cultural diversity programs and the international Jewish organizations differ substantially, both aim to cultivate Jewish religiosity by promoting an essentialist view of Jewish identity. The objectives of the diversity programs can be traced to ideas about ethnicity that serve to justify Croatia's political agenda; the objectives of the international organizations stem from a perceived crisis in Jewish identity maintenance. Both groups share an emphasis on the religious aspects of Jewish identity that has had a polarizing effect both within Jewish communities in Croatia and between Croatian Jews and non-Jews.

## NOTES

1. As we saw in earlier chapters, local and transnational organizations catered to a variety of humanitarian and social needs that eventually transformed modern Jewish life. Their purpose was largely based on providing aid to those in need of assistance. Similar to other humanitarian social movements in the nineteenth and twentieth centuries, the founders of the transnational Jewish organizations were primarily acculturated liberals, often described as the beneficiaries of the Jewish emancipation era. Most organizations

were interested in pursuing social equality for Jews and other analogous causes associated with civil liberties and social welfare. Organizations such as the World Jewish Congress (WJC) continue to provide assistance to Jews across political and religious spectra. For example, the WJC and several other Jewish organizations have been instrumental in mobilizing German and Swiss reparations to Holocaust survivors. Such organizations have also taken on the task of revitalizing Jewish communities in postcommunist countries.

2. Croatia's establishment of diplomatic ties with Israel in 1998 contrasted with Yugoslavia's official pro-Arab, anti-Zionist policy. Even though Yugoslavia was among the first nations to recognize the State of Israel in 1948, its official policy supported the Palestinian national cause. During the Yom Kippur War in October 1973, six years after the country's diplomatic break with Israel in 1967, Yugoslavia aligned herself with the Arab world, while publicly equating Zionism with racism. Despite Yugoslav foreign politics, Jewish communities in Yugoslavia continued to nourish their ties with Israel. With the new regime in Croatia, official diplomatic ties with Israel were established. The ties between Israel and Croatia are viewed as desirable for several reasons. Diplomacy is thought to improve trade relations and the tourist industry, and to mitigate Croatia's infamous role during World War II.

For many Croatian Jews, support for the State of Israel historically has been a significant expression of Jewish secular identity. At the time of my research, different means for supporting Israel existed, such as specialized week-long seminars on topics related to Jewish cultural history, "working vacations" at collective farms, Yeshiva and other study abroad programs, and the kibbutz experience. With the exception of the religious study program, these events came to a halt as the Israeli-Palestinian conflict intensified.

# Concluding Thoughts

This study has focused on the *renewed survival* of Jewish community life in postcommunist Croatia and the multifaceted strategies employed by intercultural Jews in refashioning the significance of the Jewish community. I have explored these phenomena in part against the backdrop of what some may argue are abstract theoretical debates—notably, the disappearance thesis and its opponents, and the clash between humanists and traditionalists. However, as I have argued, the issues at stake in these debates are hardly mere theoretical epiphenomena. Rather, they express real life concerns that shape the intercultural reality of community life for Croatian Jews, and which are played out in multifarious ways (in both concrete and abstract terms) through the spatial and social organization of the ŽOZ. At the end of the day, the ethnohistoric narratives of the community members reveal that Jewish community life in Croatia manifests itself both through humanist expressions as well as through a strict adherence to Jewish tradition (and all manner of variation in between). Indeed, it is precisely this variation and tension that characterizes the vigor with which Jewish identity is continually renewed and redefined in postcommunist Croatia.

As I argued in the introduction, if the disappearance thesis is correct, Jewish identity and community life should be eroding, or at least in serious decline—particularly in places such as Croatia, where intercultural Jews have been said to be assimilating into the mainstream fabric since the nineteenth century. This thesis is supported by the emancipation and acculturation trends that prevailed in Jewish Croatian society prior to the Holocaust and during Tito's Yugoslavia (where one's association with citizenship rather than with one's "roots" was encouraged). Yet the disintegration of Yugoslavia, communism, and the longstanding debates over the meaning of the Jewish community refute this prediction. Each provides a solid example of Jewish community participation becoming increasingly more important during contested nationalisms, in the postcommunist period, and throughout Jewish community revival movements.

We have seen examples of the conflict between integrationist and traditionalist views throughout Jewish Croatian history. The ethnohistoric record informs us that integrationists maintained their Jewishness and alliance to the Jewish community, despite secularization trends, communism, and the cultural integration that came to characterize Jewish community life in Croatia. Although there is scant historic documentation of these debates, it is nevertheless clear that the disparate communities participated in different social spheres. For example, the smaller contingent of Orthodox Jews rented separate rooms for worship, maintained separate burial sites, and generally disassociated themselves from the larger humanist-oriented community.

Historic accounts further reveal that humanist Jews became active in Croatian economic, cultural, and political life due to their relative early emancipation and cultural integration. Urban expansion in the nineteenth and early twentieth centuries helped sustain a Jewish professional and intellectual class in the capital. Throughout this period, Jews were integrated but not assimilated. This occurred in part because they were involved in Jewish social, political, and cultural organizations and had different outlets for Jewish identification (e.g., Zionism and antifascism).

Croatian Jews were further integrated during Tito's Yugoslavia due to the *Partisan*-led fight against fascism and Yugoslavia's official anti-Zionist position. Although Jews were treated fairly under Tito's regime and viewed as fellow Yugoslavs, Yugoslavia's anti-Zionist political position actively discouraged the expression of separate cultural identities. Thus, Jewish community life in Tito's Croatia continued, but was far from vibrant. In particular, there was no spiritual leader, or *hevra kadesha*, during this period, nor did members have the wealth of options for expressing Jewish community life as they do today.

The circumstances that came to characterize Jewish community life during Tito's Yugoslavia changed in the 1990s—a period during which Jews were once again positioned as *outsiders* and potential enemies of the Croatian national cause. The renewed survival of Croatian Jews served as a symbolic reminder of the atrocities committed by the Croatian *Ustaša* regime in 1941–1945. Jews in Croatia during the transition period, although small in number, appeared threatening to Croatian sovereignty because of Jewish association with the *Partisans*, communism, Croatia's notorious *Ustaša* past, and the imaginary Jewish lobby. Yet in the late 1990s, Croatia responded to these developments by establishing diplomatic ties with Israel and by supporting Croatian Jews through government-sponsored cultural diversity campaigns— activities that reflect Croatia's desire to be included in the European Union.

Disparate ideas about the ŽOZ's relationship with the wider public, the Croatian government, and the role of the ŽOZ rabbi continue to be central to the integrationist/traditionalist debates. This notwithstanding, community members can at least agree that *a* rabbi is needed to secure the survival of the ŽOZ. The majority of the ŽOZ community understands the rabbi's role to be that of an educator and public relations representative, negotiating the ŽOZ's relationship with the Croatian government. This view conflicts with that of the traditionalists, who view the rabbi's role as that of a religious leader and mediator between the Orthodox Jewish world and the ŽOZ.

Integrationists and traditionalists are further divided over the form and function of the future *Praška* space. For the integrationists, the space promises to release the community from various obligations to the Croatian government and international aid organizations. Accordingly, their proposal for developing the *Praška* space includes the establishment of a cultural center and museum as well as an underground parking garage and commercial office spaces. Integrationists also express concern for educating the general public about the Jewish community's past, present, and future—an impulse that is at odds with the sentiments of the traditionalists, who advocate resurrecting a replica of Klein's synagogue for the purpose of religious observance and as a monument to the ŽOZ's past. Indeed, traditionalists regard the integrationists' desire for independence as undermining the Jewish community's prospects for long-term survival and viability.

The recent developments and debates between traditionalists and integrationists over the *Praška* space forecast a relationship between the Jewish community and Croatian society based on cooperation and coming to terms with Croatia's *Ustaša* past. For integrationists, a public dialogue concerning the *Praška* space would increase public awareness of Croatia's role during the Holocaust and the destruction of the synagogue. Thus, for integrationists, the *Praška* space can provide a point of entry for imagining the future of the Jewish community, while at the same time serving to educate the general public about Jewish Croatian history. This is epitomized by the dialogue concerning the parking lot in *Praška*—a space which, for integrationists, serves both to memorialize the past and to construct the future of the Jewish community.

The potential of physical space to serve as a vehicle through which Jewish identity and community life is nurtured and reproduced is nowhere as clear as in the *Palmotićeva*, where the ŽOZ is currently housed. The array of activities offered there helps to facilitate social interaction among members, while providing them with the resources to express Jewish culture through participation in activities such as folkloric dance, ceramics, foreign language classes, and the various programs organized by the *Miroslav Salom Freiberger* cultural society.

Recent changes to the physical space of the ŽOZ have played an important role in transforming the image of the community in the eyes of its members as well as the general Croatian public. Notably, the heightened security has created the misperception of the ŽOZ as an insular community. Yet the refurbished *klub*, robust offices, large conference rooms, and the array of programs offered at the center have made the *općina* more inviting to interested and prominent outsiders and have given the ŽOZ an aura of institutional legitimacy.

This feature of Jewish community in Croatia is not without historical precedent. For Croatian Jews, the notion of community has long signified belonging to Jewish societies and voluntary associations. In the absence of the continuous face-to-face interaction that characterizes *shtetl* life, Croatian Jews often have found community through social interaction. The community that emerges as a result of participation in various clubs and societies is therefore voluntary and social/political rather than obligatory and steeped in religious tradition. Indeed, for the Croatian Jews, community continues to be defined through friendship networks and various social affiliations, including participation in religious observance.

The meaning of Jewish community is also transformed through the construction of insiders and outsiders—a process which inevitably shapes the boundaries of any community. For example, the postcommunist secularization of Jewish identity closely parallels Roman Catholic Croat identities, which are connected to the construction of nationhood in Croatia and devoid of strict adherence to Catholic observance. Moreover, as with traditionalist Jews, Croat churchgoers are often pejoratively referred to as "newly composed" Catholics. We saw a number of examples of this insider/outsider dichotomy in the passages concerning the *novo-komponirani Židovi* and *Yugonostalgics*.

The disintegration of Yugoslavia and the emergence of the Croatian nation-state provided additional possibilities for constructing the meaning of Jewish community life. Yet more possibilities are presented by the recent resurgence of Croatian nationalism and the changing meaning of ethnicity in Croatian society. For example, some feel that Jewish identification and ŽOZ affiliation have become attractive options in light of the construction of Jews as outsiders and potential enemies of Croatian nationalism. This sentiment is intensified by Croatia's tolerance of neofascism and its unwillingness to openly address its notorious *Ustaša* past.

The predominantly secular conception of Jewishness encouraged by this development is reflected in the attitudes of community members toward their newly appointed spiritual leader. Most members agree that the presence of such a leader has great value, even though they continue to understand engagement in Jewish community life as independent of the practice of Judaism.

In the introduction, I discussed the notion of essentialism, which we have seen epitomized in the government-sponsored cultural diversity programs. I noted (in chapter 6) that such programs resemble the visions of international Jewish support organizations. By imagining cultural and linguistic differences in terms of ethnic others, Croatia has attempted to distance itself from the "former regime," while aligning itself closer to the West—a strategy that reflects Croatia's unstable economic future. Jewish support organizations also seek to cultivate an essentialist image of Jewish community, but in the service of the (very different) goal of securing the continuation of Jewish community in east-central Europe.

International Jewish support organizations mistakenly suppose that the future of the Croatian Jewish community depends upon the successful promotion of an essentialist image of Jewish identity. Cultural diversity programs sponsored by the Croatian Ministry of Culture are likewise premised on the view that Jews must be submerged in tradition and religion. National as well as (some) international programs support Jewish identity maintenance by reifying differences between cultural groups and exaggerating the importance of religious consciousness. They do not, however, seek to promote a tolerant multicultural society for its own sake or to help Croatian Jews assert Jewish community life and identity on their own terms.

Essentialism is also at the heart of the traditionalist view of Jewish identity and community life, which is in conflict with the primarily humanistic worldviews of the Croatian Jews themselves. More specifically, the religious elements of the essentialist view are at odds with the complex and often contradictory ways in which Jewish identity in Croatia is expressed. Indeed, restricting the meaning of Jewish community to a singular version of Jewishness would defeat the very meaning of community for many ŽOZ members.

The inability to acknowledge the dynamic and contingent character of Jewish identity is often due to plain inattention to such facts. In particular, the notion of an inevitable assimilation of ethnic and religious identity looks implausible in light of facts recorded in national censuses (1952–2001), such as fluctuations in ethnic and religious affiliation as well as in ŽOZ membership. By taking seriously the historic record and the narratives of the community members, we can see the thoroughly contextual nature of Jewish identity construction, along with its contingency on the surrounding sociocultural environment. This discourages the temptation to regard the lifespan of a community as historically fixed.

Adherence to an essentialist picture of Jewish identity is not simply a theoretical mistake. Visions and predictions of what Jewish identity should be have unpredictable consequences for the Croatian Jews. Rather than forecasting the future of Jewish identities and Jewish community life in Croatia, it is more useful to incorporate a view of culture and history into a framework that would ultimately lead to a better understanding of the mutable nature of identity negotiation and renegotiation. The uses of history, local, and larger sociocultural forces—the meaning makers—emphasize the dynamic nature of identity politics beyond the restricted notion of genealogical descent, where the image of fixed and primordial identities is found.

It should be emphasized, however, that while individuals are always capable of creating and transforming individualized meanings of cultural identity, cultural identity negotiation is never a completely random process that is meaningless to outsiders. Cultural identities are a product of time, space, and a collective imagining. In light of this, Croatian Jews negotiate their cultural identities primarily through humanistic values and membership in social organizations. The organizations are important precisely because Jewish community life in Croatia was never confined to Jewish neighborhoods or synagogues.

We have seen that there are a number of motivations behind the self-identification choices of intercultural Croatian Jews, and just as many reasons why Croatian intercultural Jews regard Jewish identity as an attractive option. Part of the answer lies in the particular history of Croatian Jews during the Holocaust and the repositioning of Jews as *outsiders* during the xenophobic cultural milieu of Tuđman's Croatia. Individuals with no personal history of Jewish culture responded to the xenophobic 1990s and the collapse of a cultural milieu that placed the politics of Brotherhood and Unity at the forefront of its political rhetoric through symbolic essentialism. The parents of such individuals did not want to recall their memories of the Holocaust and experiences of anti-Semitism, or did not wish to disclose their Jewish background because of their commitment to Yugoslavia. However, their children and grandchildren did so with gusto. Those who embraced these positions can be found on both sides of the traditionalist/integrationist divide.

Another part of the answer lies in the fact that many intercultural Jews feel a sense of loss in not belonging to a particular heritage. Relying on symbolic essentialism as a surrogate is a strategy for achieving a sense of connection to something larger than themselves, despite the risk of estrangement from family and others. Another equally powerful strategy is to identify as a "citizen of the world." Indeed, these strategies reflect my own life's trajectory, which has been wrought with a craving for community and home as well as a heightened awareness of my own *outsider* status in the United States, my chosen home for most of my adult life.

No one can know or predict with certainty what the future for the Croatian Jews holds. Yet the idea that Jewish identity is fixed and unchanging, or that it unfolds along a historically determined trajectory, is simply inconsistent with the narratives of the ŽOZ members themselves. Jewish community life can never be understood as stable or incontestable; rather, its meaning is continually revised. Contra the disappearance thesis, if there is a real crisis facing Croatian Jews it is the institutionalized disregard for the multiple and diverse versions of Jewish community life that have coexisted for centuries. It is my sincere wish that Croatian Jews continue to embody a commitment to the diversity of Jewish community life in Croatia, where humanist and traditionalist visions coexist through tolerance and renewed survival.

# Epilogue

In May 2005 I received an e-mail informing me that the ŽOZ board had decided not to renew Rabbi Kotel's contract. His yearly contract renewal had been up for debate since he first started his appointment in 1998. Thirteen of the twenty-five board members voted against renewal, eleven voted for retaining him at his current position, and one vote was undecided. The next e-mail I received stated that Kotel and his supporters were "fighting back" and that "people as high up as the president of Croatia expressed support for the rabbi." I received this just as I was about to submit my manuscript to Lexington Books and had already planned a trip to Croatia in the middle of June to get a new research project off the ground. I asked Brian Romer, my editor, if I could include an epilogue to my manuscript if there was a story to tell. There was.

Upon my arrival in mid-June I found the ŽOZ in a war zone. I did not have to ask about the rabbi's possible departure: it was the only thing people wanted to talk about. One of the consequences of "fighting back" was that about 160 signatures were collected in support of renewing the rabbi's contract. Another was that the details of the conflict were publicized through an internet blog entitled *judenrat* (http://judenrat.blog.hr/), which means "Jewish council" in German, or "Jewish war" in Croatian (*rat* means "war" in Croatian).

On June 28th, a meeting (a gripe session, actually, and apparently the first in many years) had been organized to talk about the board's decision. Although the meeting was restricted to ŽOZ members, its outcome stretched far beyond the walls of the ŽOZ. Just days after the meeting, daily newspapers such as *Novi List*, *Jutarni List*, and *Vjesnik* wrote about the ongoing disputes, including the rumors about the potential closing of the kindergarten. The deep-seated individual rivalries between the ŽOZ management and the rabbi, and the chasm between the humanist and traditionalist constituencies, had erupted into fierce debates about the renewal of the rabbi's contract. These rivalries were further complicated when atheist and agnostic (or non-traditionalist) community members signed a petition in support of the rabbi.

There were major disagreements about the potential replacement of the rabbi—an issue to which I shall return—but by far the most critical issue of contention was the role of the ŽOZ's management, and particularly the president, in social and financial affairs. In fact, a good number of the 160 signatures collected in support of the rabbi were from people who hardly knew the man and had never even entered the synagogue.

Why, I wondered, would members who rarely or never attend synagogue services, who are not particularly interested in Judaism, and who have ridiculed the rabbi's views, sign a petition in favor of renewing his contract? Part of the answer, I soon learned, was that support for the rabbi was understood as taking a stand against the alleged corruption of the ŽOZ management and the continued debates about the form and function of the *Praška* space. A number of prominent ŽOZ members felt that the management should be "brought to justice" for financial misconduct, corruption, and protectionism. Allegations brought against particular board members ranged from charges of pocketing funds from the *Praška* parking lot to patronage (notably, replacing qualified ŽOZ staff with friends and relatives with little experience and insufficient qualifications). Another part of the answer had to do with the widespread belief that the ŽOZ will not receive another spiritual leader if Rabbi Kotel leaves. (We have already seen in previous chapters that a spiritual leader is not only considered necessary for the education of the ŽOZ's youngest members, but of utmost importance for the public persona of the ŽOZ.)

Those in favor of terminating the rabbi's contract believe that the rabbi caused divisions and discord in the ŽOZ community. They feel that his salary is too high and that he has placed too many unrealistic demands on a basically secular community. The rabbi has been said to have challenged the ŽOZ's managerial style and to have spread rumors about its moral character. Although the ŽOZ recognizes the need for a spiritual leader, those who oppose renewal are in favor of having a different rabbi serve the ŽOZ. The management pointed out that the *Kultureno Društvo Miroslav Šalom Freiberger* no longer invites the rabbi to give public lectures because his presentations have been described as being of "poor quality" and "nonintellectual." The rabbi's embarrassing creationist views have been criticized at length. Clearly, views about the rabbi's position in the ŽOZ as well as his moral character are divided. On the one hand, the rabbi has been portrayed as an unscholarly profiteer and someone who has brought contention to the ŽOZ.

On the other hand, the picture of a kind-hearted, tolerant, and well-connected man seems to flourish both within and outside the ŽOZ.

I was told a number of different stories that reflected these views. Although the rabbi has always maintained the image of a do-gooder among his original supporters, nontraditionalist members have also begun to see him in a positive light. For example, Ada, a sworn atheist, told me how the rabbi called a prestigious university in England after her son (an aspiring physicist) was denied entry. She happily signed the petition against the board's decision, believing that her son currently studies in England due to the rabbi's "personal connections." I was also told that over the years the rabbi had become much more tolerant of agnostics and members of other faiths. Although he refuses to enter a Christian place of worship when invited to interfaith gatherings or to participate in ecumenical burial rites upon request of the family members of the deceased, he has at the same time befriended Šefko Omerbašić, the chief spiritual leader of the Muslim communities in Croatia and Slovenia, and thereby spearheaded a much needed dialogue between Jews and Muslims. I was also told that Rabbi Kotel befriended President Stjepan Mesić, who publicly denounced the board's decision. (The office of Prime Minister Ivo Sanader, however, declined to comment on the situation.) Along with these remarkable personal connections, the rabbi has also received support from the European Rabbinate in Brussels, which purportedly asked Sanader to intervene on Kotel's behalf.

In short, the tiny Jewish community in Croatia has once again become newsworthy. Sanader's recent visit to Israel and Yad Veshem, Israel's Holocaust memorial, emphasizes the flourishing diplomatic relations between the two nation states. After all, they have more than Croatia's tiny Jewish population in common. Both have had leaders who ruled on exclusivist platforms and both have a growing religious right contingent. In "Openness of Society: Croatia 2005," a recent report submitted by the Open Society Institute in Zagreb, Croatia was pronounced the most Catholic country in Europe. With that observation are detailed examples of conservative values regarding sexuality and reproductive rights. It is hardly surprising, then, that an Orthodox rabbi has received support from Croatia's politicians and spiritual leaders.

But there are other issues at play. Croatian Jews are no longer viewed by the general public as an exotic minority with curious cultural practices or as *Yugonostalgics* and Serb sympathizers. Instead, they have been viewed as "cultured upstanding citizens" from whom one could learn a thing or two. Of course, these stereotypes could be as destructive for the Jewish community and individual Jews as the ones that were popular during Tuđman. That said, Croatian Jews have become *Croatians* in the popular imagination, who worship the *same* God as the Catholics.

To his credit, Kotel has taken this national and international support in stride and has maintained—as did ŽOZ's president Ognjen Kraus—that his contract renewal is an *internal* ŽOZ community matter. But it is uncertain whether the ŽOZ's affairs are going to remain community matters at a moment in history when Croatia is seeking to join the European Union, finance the rebuilding of the *Praška* space, nourish diplomatic relations with Israel, and generally protect "her" Jews.

I was also told stories about the ŽOZ management, which has been portrayed as a group of corrupt individuals, "professional Jews," who have monopolized the Jewish community and placed friends and family members in positions of power. Management is said to have ignored the appeals of the observant constituency and sought to profit from its privileged position in the community. Perhaps the most serious accusation is that individuals have pocketed funds intended for the ŽOZ community. The rental of the *Praška* parking lot was often cited as a prime example of corruption, even though management's opponents claim that many more examples of corruption exists for which they intend to bring suit.

There are many examples of protectionism. One is the idea that Rabbi Kotel would be replaced by Luciano Prelevi, a kind, robust man in his early fifties who was sent to an Israeli Yeshiva in 1999 for rabbinical studies. It was reasoned that "Luciano won't make any fuss for the management and keep the atheists happy."

Luciano was one of the first people I met when I began fieldwork in 1997. I remember him as a deeply spiritual, generous man with a healthy sense of skepticism about the management and much Judaic writing. The ŽOZ management told me that Luciano's education—sponsored in part by the ŽOZ— was provided for the sole purpose that he might serve as the ŽOZ's spiritual leader. Yet when I asked the management several years ago whether Lucino would eventually be employed by the ŽOZ, they declined to comment. Several months prior to the board's decision, however, Luciano was invited to participate in a series of public presentations at the ŽOZ. The presentations, organized by the *Miroslav Šalom Freiberger*, were aimed to reacquaint him with the ŽOZ community. They were also meant as an informal evaluation of his credentials. I was told that Luciano's presentations were poorly attended, but generally well received.

Sometime after Luciano's visit to Croatia in the spring, various rumors about his moral character began to surface. He was said to have stolen a Torah and driven a car on Sabbath. Luciano was asked to leave the first Yeshiva he attended in Jerusalem. He soon joined another Yeshiva, from which he is supposed to graduate this autumn. Yet a letter, read at the meeting, from the Yeshiva where Luciano currently studies, revealed that he would not receive a rabbinical degree but rather a degree that would allow him to function as a religious educator.

A conversation with the management confirmed that the ŽOZ had suffered much less from financing Luciano's education than from the turmoil and social unrest caused by Rabbi Kotel. The management informed me that they feel strongly about the community having a spiritual leader who "better suits the mentality of the ŽOZ and not someone who enforces ideas foreign to Croatian Jews."

Consistent throughout all these stories is the view that either the rabbi or management is somehow profiting at the expense of the community. Such a view lies at the cultural heart of Croatia's postcommunist political economy. During the former Yugoslavia, social positions and political advancement were often achieved through "personal connections." Although these connections were considered part of everyday life, they were also viewed as suspect because a person profiting from her personal connections did so at the expense of someone else. Thus, although personal connections are no longer viewed as contrary to the ideals of Brotherhood and Unity, they continue to capture the experience of postcommunism in Croatia—the rabbi has most certainly learned to abide by them.

Unsurprisingly, humanist/traditionalist debates within the Jewish community have continued and further unexpected divisions have surfaced that point to the continued malleability of cultural identities and community life. As in the past, the traditionalist contingent has remained small (recall that in the late 1930s when the Jewish community in Zagreb had 11,000 members, only about 140 individuals identified as Orthodox observers). What is different today is that the traditionalist contingent has not yet been in the position to maintain a separate lifestyle. Another difference is that ŽOZ politics—far from being an internal affair—have increasingly become of national and even international concern. This trend places the tiny community of Croatian Jews alongside other Jewish communities in postcommunist countries that have witnessed *identity reform* in response to external social pressures.

On the community-based level, the divisions have played out in the social organization of the ŽOZ, its spiritual leadership and management, and the debates about the future of the *Praška* space. Far from disintegrating or disappearing, the ŽOZ seems to be invigorated through these debates. The only serious crisis facing the ŽOZ today is an indifference of the manifold expressions of Jewish community life in Croatia. If the ŽOZ is to continue to flourish, its members, managerial staff, and future spiritual leaders must strive to embrace the diversity within the Jewish community and look for ways to coexist in the globalizing Jewish village.

# Glossary

*aliyah*: (Hebrew) Ascending; immigration to Israel

Ante Pavelić: Commander in chief of the *Ustaša* party (1941–1945)

Bileće: Croatian's first concentration camp established in the 1940s

*Bratstvo i Jedinstvo*: (Croatian) Brotherhood and Unity

Croat: Member of a Roman Catholic ethnocultural group

Croatian: Citizen of Croatia

denationalization: Process of return of property seized during communism

Family Sabbath: Monthly social gathering at the on the ŽOZ

Franjo Klein: Architect who designed the synagogue located in *Praška* 7 and destroyed in 1941

Franjo Tuđman: First president of postcommunist Croatia (1991–2000)

*Halacha*: (Hebrew) Jewish religious law

*Haskalah*: (Hebrew) Jewish Enlightenment

HDZ (*Hrvatska Demokratska Zajednica*): (Croatian) Croatian Democratic Union

*hevra kadisha*: (Hebrew) Burial society

*Hrvatsko Proljeće:* (Croatian) Croatian Spring

Humanitätsverein: (German) A humanitarian Jewish organization established in 1846

Jasenovac: The largest and most infamous death camp in Croatia (1941–1945)

Jeri klub: (Croatian) Seniors' social club active at the ŽOZ

Josip Broz Tito: Commander in chief of the *Partisans* and the president of Yugoslavia (1945–1980)

*Judaica*: Jewish religious artifacts

*klub*: (Croatian) Large room on the second floor of the ŽOZ where most of the social life occurs

Ljudevit Gaj: Led the first nationalist movement in Croatia in the nineteenth century

Illyrian project: Sociopolitical separatist movement that resulted in the Kingdom of Yugoslavia after World War I in 1918

*madriha*: (Hebrew) Educator of Jewish culture

*Makabiada*: (Hebrew) Jewish Olympic Games

*menorah*: (Hebrew) Seven-branch candle holder used in religious ceremonies

*mezuzah*: (Hebrew) Prayer affixed in a holder placed on Jewish doorposts *mikvah*: (Hebrew) A ritual bathhouse used by observant Jews

Mirogoj: The main cemetery in Zagreb

*Miroslav Salom Freiberger*: Cultural society named after ŽOZ's rabbi Miroslav Salom Freiberger who died in Auschwitz in 1943

Motek: (Hebrew) Cute or small; a youth publication circulating among ŽOZ members

NDH (*Neovisna Drzava Hrvatska*): (Croatian) Independent State of Croatia (1941–1945)

*Neologue*: (Greek) New thought; a branch of Judaism associated with the Jewish Enlightenment that originating in Hungary in 1860

*novo-komponirani Židovi*: (Croatian) Newly composed Jews

omladinki klub: (Croatian) Youth social club active at the ŽOZ

*općina*: (Croatian) The physical community center or the abstract "Jewish community"

Pirovac: Place on the Adriatic coast were a Jewish summer camp is held

self-managing socialism: Political ideology associated with Tito and Yugoslavia

*Trg Žrtava Fašizma*: (Croatian) Victims of Fascism Square

*Ustaša*: Fascist political party that came to power during Independent Croatia (1941–1945)

Ženska Sekcija: (Croatian) The Women's Division, a social activities group active in the ŽOZ

Židovska Smotra: (Croatian) *Jewish Review*, a newspaper

# Bibliography

Amyot, Robert P., and Lee Singelman. 1996. "Jews without Judaism? Assimilation and Jewish Identity in the United States," *Social Science Quarterly*, 77, no. 1: 177–89.

Arendt, Hannah H. 1963. *Eichmann in Jerusalem*. New York: Viking Press.

Azoulay, Katya Gibel. 1997. *Black, Jewish, and Interracial: It's Not the Color of Your Skin, but the Race of Your Kin, and Other Myths of Identity*. Durham, N.C.: Duke University Press.

Bakalian, Anny. 1993. *Armenian Americans: From Being to Feeling Armenian*. New Brunswick, N.J.: Transaction Publishers.

Bakić-Hayden, Milica, and Robert M. Hayden. 1992. "Orientalist Variations on the Theme Balkans: Symbolic Geography in Recent Yugoslav Cultural Politics." *Slavic Review*, 51, no. 1: 1–15.

Barack Fishman, Sylvia. 2004. *Double or Nothing: Jewish Families and Mixed Marriage*. Lebanon, N.H.: Brandies University Press.

Barth, Frederik. 1979. *Ethnic Groups and Boundaries: The Social Organization of Culture Difference*. Bergen, Norway: Universitetsforlaget.

Bateson, Gregory. 1979. *Mind and Nature: A Necessary Unity*. New York: Dutton.

Bedenko, Vladimir. 1998. "*Domus Juderom u Srednjovjekovnom Zagrebu.*" In *Dva Stoljeća Povijesti i Kulture Židova u Zagrebu i Hrvatskoj*, edited by Ognjen Kraus. Zagreb: Židovska Općina Zagreb.

Behar, Ruth. 1996. *The Vulnerable Observer: Anthropology That Breaks Your Heart*. Boston: Beacon Press.

Behar, Ruth, and Deborah A. Gordon, eds. 1995. *Women Writing Culture*. Berkeley: University of California Press.

Berdahl, Daphne, Matti Bunzl, and Martha Lampand, eds. 2000. *Altering States: Ethnographies of the Transition in Eastern Europe and Russia*. Ann Arbor: University of Michigan Press.

Bershtel, Sara, and Allen Graubard. 1992. *Saving Remnants: Feeling Jewish in America*. New York: The Free Press.

Borneman, John, and Jeffery Peck. 1995. *Sojourners: The Return of German Jews and the Question of Identity*. Lincoln: University of Nebraska.

Bowman, Glen. 1994. "Xenophobia, Fantasy and the Nation: The Logic of Ethnic Violence in Former Yugoslavia." In *Anthropology of Europe: Identity and Boundaries in Conflict*, edited by Virginia A. Goddard, Joseph R. Llobera, and Chris Shore. Providence, R.I.: Berg Publishers.

Brass, Paul R. 1991. *Ethnicity and Nationalism: Theory and Comparison*. New Delhi: Sage Publishers.

Breuilly, John. 1994. "The Sources of Nationalist Ideology." In *Nationalism,* edited by John Hutchinson and Anthony D. Smith. Oxford: Oxford University Press.

Brubaker, Roger. 1996. *Nationalism Reframed: Nationhood and the National Question in the New Europe*. Cambridge and New York: Cambridge University Press.

Buckser, Andrew. 2003. *After the Rescue: Jewish Identity and Community in Contemporary Denmark*. New York: Palgrave Macmillan.

Bunzl, Matti. 2004. *Symptoms of Modernity: Jews and Queers in Late-Twentieth-Century Vienna*. Berkeley: University of California Press.

Burawoy, Michael, and Katherine Verdery, eds. 1999. *Uncertain Transition: Ethnographies of Change in the Postsocialist World*. Lanham, Md.: Rowman & Littlefield Publishers.

Clifford, James, and George Marcus, eds. 1986. *Writing Culture: The Poetics and Politics of Ethnography*. Berkeley: University of California Press.

Cohen, Anthony. 1983. *The Symbolic Construction of Community*. New York and London: Travistock.

Connor, Walker. 1994. *Ethnonationalism: The Quest for Understanding*. Princeton, N.J.: Princeton University Press.

Cviic, Chistopher. 1995. *The Balkans*. London: Wellington House.

DellaPergola, Sergio. 1994. "An Overview of the Demographic Trends of European Jewry." In *Jewish Identities in the New Europe,* edited by Jonathan Webber. London and Washington, D.C.: Published for the Oxford Center for Postgraduate Hebrew Studies, Littman Library of Jewish Civilization.

Denitch, Bette. 1994. "Dismembering Yugoslavia: Nationalist Ideologies and the Symbolic Revival of Genocide." *American Ethnologist*, 21, no. 2: 367–90.

Drakulić, Slavenka. 1997. *Café Europa: Life After Communism*. New York and London: W. W. Norton & Company.

Eisen, Arnold. 1994. "Rethinking Jewish Modernity" *Jewish Social Studies: History, Culture and Society*, 1, no. 1:1–21.

Eriksen, Thomas H. 1993. *Ethnicity and Nationalism: Anthropological Perspectives*. London: Pluto Press.

Finkielkraut, Alain. 1994. *The Imaginary Jew*. Lincoln and London: University of Nebraska Press.

Freidenreich, Harriet Pass. 1984. *The Jews of Yugoslavia: a Quest for Community*. Philadelphia: Jewish Publication Society of America.

Friedreich, Dean. 2003. ŽOZ, Secretary General (personal communication).

Gans, Herbert J. 1994. "Symbolic Ethnicity and Symbolic Religiosity: Towards a Comparison of Ethnic and Religious Acculturation." *Ethnic and Racial Studies*, 17, no. 4: 577–92.

Garb, Tamar, and Linda Nochlin, eds. 1995. *The Jew in the Text: Modernity and the Construction of Identity*. London: Thames and Hudson Ltd.

Gazi, Stephen. 1993. *A History of Croatia*. New York: Barnes & Noble.

Geertz, Clifford. 1973. *The Interpretation of Cultures*. New York: Basic Books.

Goldberg, David T., ed. 1994. *Multi-Culturalism: A Critical Reader*. Oxford: Blackwell.

Goldstein, Ivo. 1996. "Antisemitizam u Hrvatskoj: Korijeni, Pojava I Razvoj Anitisemitizma u Hrvatskoj." In *Antisemitizam Holokaust Antifašizam*, edited by Ognjen Kraus. Zagreb: Židovska Općina Zagreb.

————. 1998. "Zagrebačka Židovska Općina od Osnutka do 1941." In *Dva Stoljeća Povijesti i Kulture Židova u Zagrebu i Hrvatskoj*, edited by Ognjen Kraus. Zagreb: Židovska Općina Zagreb.

Goldstein, Slavko. 1998. "Židovska Općina Zagreb od 1941. do 1997. Godine." In *Dva Stoljeća Povijesti i Kulture Židova u Zagrebu i Hrvatskoj*, edited by Ognjen Kraus. Zagreb: Židovska Općina Zagreb.

Goluboff, Sascha L. 2003. *Jewish Russians: Upheavals in a Moscow Synagogue*. Philadelphia: University of Pennsylvania Press.

Gordiejew, Paul B. 1999. *Voices of Yugoslav Jewry*. Albany: State University of New York Press.

Gruber, Ruth Ellen. 2002. *Virtually Jewish: Reinventing Jewish Culture in Europe*. Berkeley: University of California Press.

Gruden, Živko. 1996. "What's in a Label and What's Behind It?" *Voice of the Jewish Communities in Croatia* (Spring): 13–15.

Hayden, Robert M. 1992. "Constitutional Nationalism in the Formerly Yugoslav Republics." *Slavic Review*, 51, no. 4: 654–82.

Horowitz, Donald L. 1985. *Ethnic Groups in Conflict*. Los Angeles: University of California Press.

Ivić, Pavele. 1986. *Srpski Narod I Njegov Jezik*. Beograd: Srpska Književna Zadruga.

Kampus, Ivan, and Igor Karaman. 1995. *Zagreb through a Thousand Years: From Ancient Settlements to Modern City*. Zagreb: Školska Knjiga.

Keller, Mose. 1966. "An Historical and Sociological Survey of European Jewry." In *Judaism Crisis Survival*, edited by Ana Rose. Paris: World Union of Jewish Students.

Kessel, Barbara. 2000. *Suddenly Jewish: Jews Raised as Gentiles Discover Their Jewish Roots*. Hanover, N.H.: Brandeis University Press.

Klajner, Milena. 1997. "Minority Legislation." In *Multicultural Reality and Perspectives in Croatia*, edited by Vjeran Katunarić. Zagreb: Interkultura.

Klein, Isaac. 1979. *A Guide to Jewish Religious Practices*. New York: The Jewish Theological Seminary of America.

Klein, Rudolf. 1998. "Sinagogalna Arhitektura na tlu Hrvatske u Kontekstu Austro-Ugarske Monarhije." In *Dva Stoljeća Povijesti i Kulture Židova u Zagrebu i Hrvatskoj*, edited by Ognjen Krauss. Zagreb: Židovska Općina Zagreb.

Knežević, Snješka. 1998. "The Zagreb Synagogue." *Voice of the Jewish Communities in Croatia* (Autumn): 30–34.

Kolar-Dimitrijević, Mira. 1998. "Prvo Dobrotvorno Društvo *Humanitaetsverein* u Zagrebu." In *Dva Stoljeća Povijesti i Kulture Židova u Zagrebu i Hrvatskoj*, edited by Ognjen Kraus. Zagreb: Židovska Općina Zagreb.

Kovač, Vlasta. 2002. "Searching for Lost Memory." *Voice of the Jewish Communities in Croatia* (Winter): 20–31.

Kraus, Ognjen. 1996. "The Jewish Community in Croatia." *Voice of the Jewish Communities in Croatia*, (Spring) 1: 4–9.

Krieger, Susan. 1991. *Social Science and the Self: Personal Essays on an Art Form*. New Brunswick, N.J.: Rutgers University Press.

Lengel Krizman, Narcisa. 1996. "Logori za Židove u NDH." In *Antisemitizam Holokaust Antifašizam*, edited by Ognjen Kraus. Zagreb: Židovska Općina Zagreb.

Mayer, Egon. 1985. *Love & Tradition: Marriage between Jews and Christians*. New York: Plenum Press.

Moore, Henrietta. 1988. *Feminism and Anthropology*. Minneapolis: University of Minnesota Press.

Petrović, Ruza. 1983. "The National Composition of the Population." *Yugoslav Survey*, no. 24: 21–34.

Ramet, Sabrina P. 1992. *Nationalism and Federalism in Yugoslavia, 1962–1991*. Bloomington: Indiana University Press.

Reinharz, Shulamit. 1992. *Feminist Methods in Social Research*. New York and Oxford: Oxford University Press.

Rohantinski, Željko, and Vojnić, Dragomir, eds. 1998. *Process of Privatization*. Zagreb: The Open Society Institute.

Rosaldo, Renato. 1989. *Culture and Truth: The Remaking of Social Analysis*. Boston: Beacon Press.

Rubin, Gale. 1975. "The Traffic in Women: Notes on the Political Economy of Sex." In *Towards an Anthropology of Women*, edited by Rarna R. Reiter. New York: Monthly Review Press.

Samary, Catherine. 1995. *Yugoslavia Dismembered*. New York: Monthly Review Press.

Schmelz, U. O., and Sergio DellaPergola. 1988. *Basic Trends in American Jewish Demography*. New York: American Jewish Committee, Institute of Human Relations.

Schweid, Eliezer. 1994. "Changing Jewish Identities in the New Europe and the Consequences for Israel." In *Jewish Identities in the New Europe*, edited by Jonathan Webber. London and Washington, D.C.: Published for the Oxford Center for Postgraduate Hebrew Studies, Littman Library of Jewish Civilization.

Sekulić, Dusko, Randy Hodson, and Garth Massey. 1994. "Who Were the Yugoslavs? Failed Sources of a Common Identity in the Former Yugoslavia." *American Sociological Review*, 59: 83–97.

Stacey, Judith. 1991. "Can There Be a Feminist Ethnography?" In *The Feminist Practice of Oral History*, edited by Sherma Gluck and Daphne Patai. New York: Routledge.

Stack, Carol B. 1996. "Writing Ethnography: Feminist Critical Practice." In *Feminist Dilemmas in Fieldwork*, edited by Diane L. Wolf. Boulder, Colo.: Westview Press.

Strčić, Petar. 1998. "Pljačka Zlata (1.065,339 kg) Zagrebackih Židova." In *Dva Stoljeća Povijesti i Kulture Židova u Zagrebu i Hrvatskoj*, edited by Ognjen Kraus. Zagreb: Židovska Općina Zagreb.

Švob, Melita. 1997. *Židovi u Hrvatskoj: Migracije i Promjene u Židovskoj Populaciji*. Zagreb: D-Graff.

Szabo, Agneza. 1998. "Židovi u Proces Modernizacije Građanskog Društva u Hrvatskoj Izmeđju 1873. i 1914. Godine." In *Dva Stoljeća Povijesti i Kulture Židova u Zagrebu i Hrvatskoj*, edited by Ognjen Kraus. Zagreb: Židovska Općina Zagreb.

Tönnies, Ferdinant. 1963. *Community and Society*. New York: Harper & Row.

Ugresić, Dubravka. 1995. *Have a Nice Day: From the Balkan War to the American Dream*. New York: Viking.

Verdery, Katherine. 1996. *What Was Socialism and What Comes Next?* Princeton, N.J.: Princeton University Press.

Webber, Jonathan, ed. 1994. *Jewish Identities in the New Europe.* London and Washington, D.C.: Published for the Oxford Center for Postgraduate Hebrew Studies, Littman Library of Jewish Civilization.

Weiner, Anita. 2003. *Renewal: Reconnecting Soviet Jewry to the Jewish People.* New York: University of America Press.

Weston, Katn. 1991. *Families We Chose.* New York: Columbia University Press.

Wolf, Diane L. 1996. "Situating Feminist Dilemmas in Fieldwork." In *Feminist Dilemmas in Fieldwork*, edited by Diane L. Wolf. Boulder, Colo.: Westview Press.

# Index

# About the Author

**Nila Ginger Hofman** is an assistant professor of anthropology at DePaul University in Chicago, Illinois. She was born in Zagreb, Croatia, in 1962 and immigrated with her family to the Netherlands in 1966. She has been teaching and conducting research amongst hidden urban populations in Chicago, including injection drug users and undocumented immigrants, since 2001. She has lived for more than twenty years in the United States. *Renewed Survival* is her first book.